Knowing Through Changing

The Evolution of Brief Strategic Therapy

Giorgio Nardone
Claudette Portelli

Crown House Publishing Limited
www.crownhouse.co.uk

First published by

Crown House Publishing Ltd
Crown Buildings, Bancyfelin, Carmarthen, Wales, SA33 5ND, UK
www.crownhouse.co.uk

and

Crown House Publishing Company LLC
4 Berkeley Street, 1st Floor, Norwalk, CT 06850, USA
www.CHPUS.com

British Library Cataloguing-in-Publication Data
A catalogue entry for this book is available
from the British Library.

10-digit ISBN 1845900154
13-digit ISBN 978-184590015-1

LCCN 2005931363

Printed and bound in the UK by
Cromwell Press
Trowbridge
Wiltshire

Contents

Foreword

Knowing Through Changing is a masterful work that presents the culmination of two decades of advancements in psychotherapy. Professor Nardone and his colleagues, using the innovative approach of brief strategic therapy, have developed highly effective and elegant treatment protocols for the most difficult of psychopathologies. From anorexia, obsessive-compulsive disorder and agoraphobia to paranoia, relational problems, and difficult children, brief strategic therapy has proven more effective than the best psychotherapies in current use around the world. The approach involves using the patient's own logic to help them overcome their problems, freeing them from long-lasting disability and reliance on medication. Like the martial art of aikido, brief strategic therapy allows the therapist to use the force of the patient's resistance to defeat entrenched psychopathologies. When these techniques are employed, seemingly miraculous effects can result in as few as 1–2 sessions, even with symptoms that have persisted, despite medication, for years of traditional therapy. This full treatment averages 10–15 sessions.

The therapeutic processes of several types of problems are presented in this book in order to demonstrate that the right strategies applied in the correct systemic order can create permanent positive changes without symptom substation or relapse. The approach is supported by years of empirical research that was rigorously conducted in Italy by Professor Nardone and his colleagues.

The approach is outlined in a clear way to demonstrate that the protocols are structured enough to facilitate the learning of the therapist and provide for their consistent and replicable application to specific patients, yet they are also flexible enough to allow for adaptation for use with virtually any problem.

Knowing Through Changing is a magnum opus in the field and a must-read for any serious practitioner of psychotherapy.

Professor Nardone has "thrown our caps over the wall" and encouraged us to follow into a new era of highly effective and efficient treatment for mental illness.

Chad Hybarger Psy.D., MFT
Clinical Director
San Diego Youth & Community Services
San Diego, California

Chapter 1

Strategic-Constructivistic Problem-Solving Theory

"Good practice does not exist without good theory."
Leonardo da Vinci

The art of changing problematic situations by applying strategic interventions that start off virtuous circles to replace vicious ones is part of a millennial tradition. In other words, *strategic problem-solving* interventions are certainly not a novelty. We find illustrious examples in antiquity, within both the Western and the Eastern cultural traditions.

We should emphasize that our use of the term *strategic problem solving* refers to a particular model of problem solving, which is based on a specific, highly advanced epistemology and logic that distinguishes this model from others.

A well-known Islamic story can help us clarify the premises of *strategic logic*, as well as what the role of a *strategic problem solver* should be.

It is told that, at his death Ali Baba, left an inheritance of 39 camels to his four sons, with the stipulation that half of the camels go to his eldest son, a quarter of them to his second son, an eighth to his third son, and a tenth to his youngest son. The four sons immediately started an intense argument about the will: how could it be possible to divide 39 camels in that manner? While the sons were animatedly discussing how to solve this dilemma, a Sufi (a wandering sage) happened to ride by on his camel. He listened to their problem, and decided to help them. He got off his camel and added it to the 39 camels. Then, as the brothers looked on in astonishment, he started to divide the camels: twenty to the eldest son, ten to the second, five to the third son, and four to the youngest. Then he got back on his camel and rode away, leaving the brothers dumbfounded.

On hearing this story, we might be left wondering, like the four brothers, if the division of the camels was made possible by some magical intervention. But the wise man did actually not perform any kind of magic: he simply applied rigorous mathematical logic by adding an x variable (as is allowed in mathematical equations) in order to make possible an otherwise impossible operation. At the end of this operation, all he did was to take back his x variable, i.e. the fortieth camel, which was his own. This rigorous type of logic makes it possible to provide a simple solution to an apparently complicated problem that would seem impossible to solve from the perspective of traditional Aristotelian logic, which relies on the premises of "true or false" or "no third value".

We believe the story of the 39 camels is a good metaphor for the attitude of a strategic problem solver. Like the wandering sage in the story, the modern *technician of change*, who sets out to reach an objective, applies his tools and professional skills and then takes them back, starting off a change process that will lead the system to evolve. However, the problem solver's strategies are not the product of a sudden spur of creativity: they are based on applying a precise and rigorous logical model of intervention. More specifically, strategic problem solving is based on a specialized branch of mathematical logic known as *strategic logic* (Elster, 1979, 1985; Da Costa, 1989a, 1989b; Nardone, Salvini, 1997; Nardone, 1998; Nardone et al., 2000).

One of the features that distinguish strategic logic from traditional types of logic is that it makes it possible to develop models of intervention based on preset objectives and the specific characteristics of the problem at hand, rather than on rigid, pre-constituted theories. In other words, we do not blindly follow some rigid, deterministic perspective that dictates how to proceed and purports to provide, *a priori*, an exhaustive description of the phenomena at hand.

In fact, even the most sophisticated theories can, if they are also highly deterministic and absolutistic, become a powerful lens that deforms the reality to which it is applied—to the detriment of truly effective interventions, because the adopted strategy will be more heavily influenced by the theory of reference than by the characteristics of the problem to be solved.

Schopenhauer pointed out the influence exercised by theory and models in people's relationship with the realities that they face. From Heisenberg's principle of indetermination to modern constructivist epistemology, it has become increasingly clear how powerful a chosen theory can be in the interpretation of the phenomena to which the theory is applied. "It is the theories that determine what we are able to observe," Einstein stated in the 1930s.

Although this awareness is now universal within modern philosophy of science, most current theoretical and methodological approaches in psychology and psychiatry, as well as psychotherapy, are still based on strong descriptive and normative theories. On the contrary, our strategic approach operates on the premise that any strong theory that establishes *a priori* strategies or interventions should be relinquished. We therefore avoid defining the nature of things, or trying to determine a definitive, universal mode of intervention. It is always the solution that adapts to the problem and not the contrary, as in most traditional models of clinical psychology and psychotherapy. In short, strategic logic wants to be flexible and tries to adapt to its object of study.

Our approach has its roots in modern constructivist epistemology, according to which there is no ontologically "true" reality, but many subjective realities that vary according to the point of view that is adopted. Reality is considered to be a product of the perspective, the instruments of knowledge, and the language by which we perceive and communicate (Salvini, 1988).

Consequently, the value of a theory depends on its ability to conceive a real intervention measured in terms of efficacy and effectiveness in solving problems. While abandoning the reassuring positivistic thesis of the existence of a "scientifically true" knowledge of reality, in strategic interventions we are concerned with identifying the most "functional" ways of knowing and acting, i.e. increasing what von Glasersfeld (1984) has called "operative awareness".

A strategic psychotherapist is not interested in discovering deep realities and the *why* of things, but only *how* things work and *how* to make them work as well as possible. Our first concern is to adapt our knowledge to the partial "realities" that we need to work on, developing strategies based on the objectives to be reached, that can adapt step by step to the evolutions of "reality".

Increasing our operative awareness, therefore, means leaving the search for the causes of events in the background and concentrating instead on increasing our capacity for strategic management of the reality that surrounds us, in order to reach our objectives. Thus, the first step is to avoid adopting deterministic positions. We do this by taking as our starting point our initial observations of the reality to be intervened upon. In order to do that, we have to orient our method of inquiry toward change, starting with the questions we ask.

According to Wittgenstein (1980), the language we use in turn uses us, in the sense that the linguistic codes that we employ to communicate reality are the same as we use in the representation and elaboration of our own perceptions. This means that different languages lead to different representations of reality.

Whether a question is asked using one linguistic code rather than another is therefore not without consequence, because the type of question asked always determines the type of answer given.

In order to have a *strategic* change, we cannot, therefore, use a linguistic code that is based on causal reconstruction: we must instead use a code that focuses on the process of change. Psychologists and/or psychiatrists who use particular diagnostic criteria to analyze a certain reality will observe a pathology that is consistent with those criteria. In other words, they will not "know" a phenomenon, but will "recognize" it because their method of inquiry is distorted by rigid codes of language and representation. As Kant observed, most of our problems derive not from the incorrect answers that we give ourselves but from the incorrect questions that we ask ourselves.

Based on what we have said so far, we will also replace the question "why?", which refers to a linear process of causality, with the question "how does it work?" By asking how a given situation "works", we avoid setting out to look for "the guilty party" and focus instead on what determines the persistence of a particular equilibrium, and how this equilibrium can be modified. This involves focusing our observation on the persistence of a problem rather than its formation, because it is on the persistence of a problem that we can intervene, not on its past formation. As the reader can easily understand, this apparently minimal difference of approach is actually a crucial aspect that distinguishes and characterizes the strategic problem-solving process.

Thus, the strategic approach represents a passage from a type of knowledge that purports to describe the reality of things (positivist and deterministic knowledge) to an operative knowledge (constructive knowledge) that enables us to manage reality as functionally as possible (Nardone, 1998).

From this point of view, the psychotherapist acts according to the advice of ancient Zen Buddhism, which identified two types of truth: "truths of essence" and "truths of error". The first, "transcendent truths", can be reached only in the afterworld, through "enlightenment"; the second type, "instrumental tools", are useful for constructing and carrying out projects in the world of objects and appearances. Every "truth of error" breaks down after being used and must be replaced by other "truths of error", which vary from case to case, in virtue of the changing realities continuously faced by all living beings (Watzlawick and Nardone, 1997).

The strategic therapist might thus be compared to an experienced seafarer in the middle of the ocean, who tries to predict and plan his actions based on the current conditions of the sea. He needs to plan for the unexpected, and be prepared to deal with it, relying on his own "operative awareness", not on having absolute control over events. Moreover, the seafarer does not and cannot know the deep truths contained in the sea, nor the reasons for its changes. And yet, with the knowledge that he does have available, which is

5

limited to "know-how", he traverses oceans and rides out storms, always adapting his actions to current developments (Nardone, 1991).

Chapter 2

The Genealogy of Brief Strategic Therapy

"The path of our life is like a mosaic, we cannot recognize and judge it
before getting to some distance away from it."
Arthur Schopenhauer

The first model of brief strategic therapy was formulated by a famous group of scientists at the Mental Research Institute in Palo Alto (Watzlawick, Weakland, and Fisch, 1974; Weakland et al., 1974). These researchers synthesized the results of their own research on communication and family therapy with Milton Erickson's technical contributions on hypnotherapy. The result was a systematic model of brief therapy that could be applied to a wide variety of disorders, with truly surprising results.

However, the pragmatic tradition and philosophy of stratagems as a key to problem solving have a much more ancient history. Strategies that still seem modern can be found, for example, in the persuasive arts of the Sophists, in the ancient practices of Zen Buddhism, and in the Chinese arts of stratagems, as well as in the ancient Greek art of Métis.[1]

Since the 1970s, brief therapy has spread almost epidemically, despite some resistance by authors attached to traditional clinical theories and practice. Many researchers and therapists have made this approach to human problems and their solutions well known internationally (Watzlawick, Weakland and Fisch, 1974; Weakland et al., 1974; De Shazer, 1982, 1984, 1985, 1988; Haley, 1963, 1976; Madanes, 1990, 1995; Nardone, 1991, 1993, 1995, 2004; Nardone and Watzlawick, 1990; Zeig and Gilligan, 1990; Cade, O'Hanlon,

---

[1] The Greek tradition of cunning intelligence, audacity and skilled abilities. It is renowned for its powers of practical wisdom.

1993; Bloom, 1995; Watzlawick, Nardone, 1997; Nardone, 2000; Nardone, Rocchi, Giannotti, 2001; Nardone, Watzlawick, 2004).

Brief strategic therapy has been developed, therefore, from its first formulations till today, initially in trends marked in some important authors' ideas and charismatic personality, then it changed showing differentiated models, which, even if keeping a common theoretical base, came to characterize themselves as clinical models and intervention techniques.

To avoid tedious repetitions, since numerous books were published on this topic, we chose to schematize the first evolution of strategic approaches with a chart (see Figure 2.1), a sort of genealogical tree of brief therapy.[2]

As seen from Figure 2.1, the approach to brief strategic therapy based on procedures of strategic intervention, from Erickson's first experiences onwards, has a branched evolution characterized by the greater emphasis given by the authors of the main models to some specific assumptions or techniques that have marked their features.

The group from the Palo Alto focused their attention on the vicious circle of the persistence of a problem. This study led the group to understand that there was a need to intervene and devise maneuvers to stop and reorganize the dysfunctional attempted solutions of the subjects which maintained and worsened the problem. In the meantime we find the communicative directivity of Haley's model and his interventions in reorganizing of power games within the family hierarchical and communicative dynamics, and the work carried out by the Milwaukee group in creating solutions from focusing on the "exception" to the problem, independently from its formation and persistency. This first phase of evolution, which lasted more than twenty years, until the end of the 1980s and early 1990s, was followed by a historical period

---

[2] In order to avoid making the text too dull, dates and quotations of authors of publications on the Brief Therapy history have been cut out. For that alone, many extra pages would have been necessary. The interested reader can find them in the complete collection of essays on this topic and full of precise bibliographical in the book by Giorgio Nardone and Paul Watzlawick (2004), *Brief Strategic Therapy*.

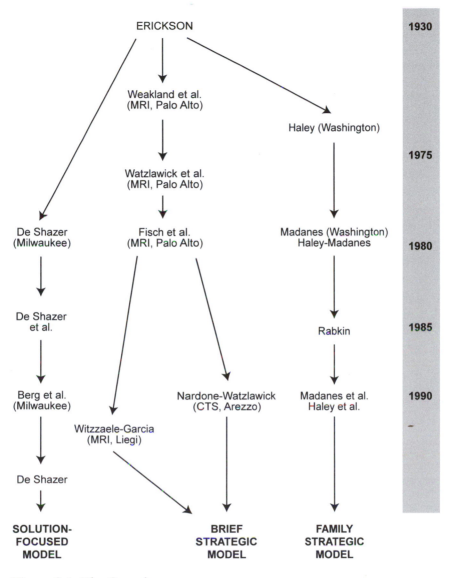

Figure 2.1. The Genealogy

characterized by the attempts of certain authors to put together approaches that would summarized the most significant contributions coming from all three traditional models of brief therapy. After this phase, characterized by a theoretical and application-oriented synthesis, the following years witnessed the development of more specific techniques with more focused directions.

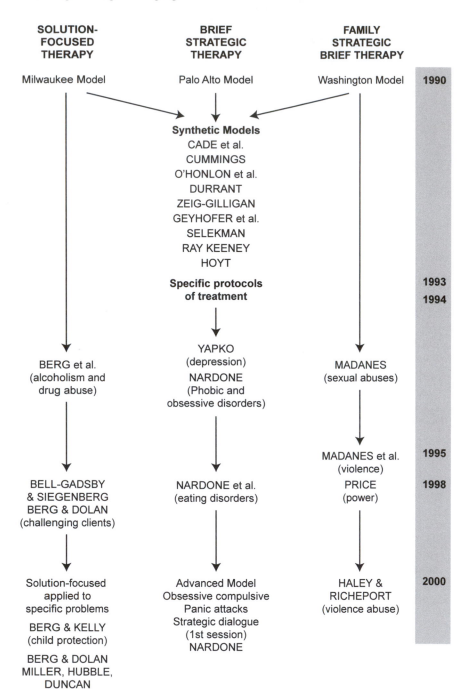

Figure 2.2

In particular, we notice the tendency to the applied study of specific strategies of therapy that were not only single techniques for recurrent forms of resistance to change, but strategic plans of an articulate therapeutic sequence studied ad hoc for particular pathologies. Also for this reason, we chose to insert another genealogical tree of brief therapy arising from the Milwaukee Model, the Palo Alto Model and the Washington Model.

From Figure 2.2, we can have the schematized representation of how from Haley–Madanes approach the therapy for sexual abuses and disorders related to violence has developed; from De Shazer's model we can observe the evolution of the treatment for drug and alcohol addicts; from Palo Alto earlier viewpoint and synthetic approaches, Nardone developed therapeutic protocols for phobic-obsessive and eating disorders and recently has evolved a strategic dialogue, which turned the first clinical session into a real intervention rather than an explicative meeting.

At this point, after having presented a simple outline of the development, from its first Ericksonian rough formulations to the building of real, theoretical, applied models and their following evolutions, we can now develop further our work: that is, the exposition of the Advanced Brief Strategic Therapy Model, developed by the group of the CTS (Strategic Therapy Center) in Arezzo, directed by one of the authors, Giorgio Nardone. This work was first carried out under the supervision of J. Weakland and P. Watzlawick and was then further developed by G. Nardone, who introduced a specific methodology of research, towards the formation of an advanced approach characterized by specific protocols of treatment for various types of pathologies.

Therapy as research, research as therapy

Since 1985, by means of an empirical experimental method, the Centro di Terapia Strategica (Strategic Therapy Center) in Arezzo, Italy, has conducted research for the development of advanced models of strategic solution-oriented brief therapy. The most important results have been the formulation of protocols for the treatment of specific types of mental disorder—mainly phobic-obsessive and eating disorders (Nardone and Watzlawick 1993; Nardone, Verbitz, and Milanese, 1999)—with high efficacy and efficiency outcomes, which were scientifically recognized to be actually the highest in the psychotherapy field (87% of solved cases in a median duration of seven sessions).

The key idea was to develop, from general models of therapy, specific protocols of treatment for particular pathologies, i.e. rigorous sequences of therapeutic maneuvers with heuristic and predictive power, capable of guiding the therapist by making use of particular therapeutic stratagems, to break the specific pathological rigidity of the disorder or problem presented. Following this first significant change, the protocols were designed in such a way as to lead the patients to reorganize their perceptive-reactive system toward a more functional balance. The focus of this laborious and prolonged work, applied to thousands of cases in a period of over ten years, was that of identifying the most adequate ways to solve each of the specific problems studied. This also led us to new assumptions regarding the structure and procedures of problem solving and regarding the maneuvers related to therapeutic relationship and language. Thus specific treatment protocols were developed, comprising specific maneuvers regarding the strategy, language and therapeutic relationship for each specific disorder or problem studied.

These protocols are rigorous yet not rigid, since they are adjustable to the answers or effects obtained from the interventions introduced—just as in a chess game, after an opening move, successive moves depend on how our adversary plays.

In a chess game, if the player manages to find moves that reveal the adversary's strategy, he is then able to attempt a formalized sequence that will lead to a final checkmate move. The same takes place in therapy: if an intervention manages to reveal the modality or persistence of the specific disorder, then the therapist can develop a specific treatment protocol that will eventually lead to the resolution of the presented problem.

In brief strategic therapy, the outcome measurement is not only carried out at the end of the therapy, but it is held at every single phase of the therapeutic process. Just as in mathematics, we look out for all possible answers to every single maneuver, and then check them out through empirical experimental procedures. Such methodology leads to a narrowing down of the possible answers (to a maximum of two or three for every single intervention), thus in this way allowing us to device the next move for each possible answer. Therefore, we proceed to obtain a measurement of the effects and predictive values for every single maneuver, and not just for the overall therapeutic process.

The *systematic process of research* carried out on various forms of psychological disorders turned out to be an important instrument of knowledge. In fact the data gathered during our research enabled us to produce an epistemological and operative model of the formation and persistence of the pathologies under study. This guided us to further improvement of solution strategies, in a sort of spiral evolution nourished by the interaction between empirical interventions and epistemological reflections, which led to the construction of specific, innovative strategies (Nardone and Watzlawick, 2004).

Applied research on our clinical work (Nardone and Watzlawick 1990; Nardone, 1993, 1995a; Fiorenza and Nardone, 1995; Nardone, Milanese and Verbitz, 1999) has enabled us to detect a series of specific models of rigid interaction between the subject and reality. These models led to the formation of specific typologies of psychological disorders, which are maintained by reiterated dysfunctional attempts to solve the problem. This leads to the formation of what we call a pathogenic "system of perceptions and reactions",[3] which expresses itself as an obstinate perseverance in using supposedly productive strategies that have worked for similar problems in the past but that now, instead, make the problem reverberate (Nardone and Watzlawick, 1990).

Therefore, the evolved model of the strategic approach goes beyond the nosographic classifications of psychiatry and clinical

---

[3] By *perceptive-reactive system* we mean an individual's redundant modalities of perception and reaction toward reality. These are expressed in the functioning of the three independent fundamental typologies of relationship: between Self and Self, Self and others, and Self and the world (Nardone, 1991).

psychology[4] by adopting a model of the categorization of problems in which the construct "perceptive-reactive" system replaces the traditional categories of mental pathology.[5]

This goes against the current tendencies of many therapists who had initially rejected the traditional nosographic classifications, but who now seem to want to resume their use. From our point of view, classification is just another attempt to force the facts, an attempt to make patients fit in one's theory of reference, without holding any concrete operative value.

In light of these theoretical epistemological assumptions, it seems essential to make what we call an "operative" diagnosis (or "diagnosis intervention") when defining a problem, instead of a merely "descriptive" diagnosis. Descriptive perspectives such as that of the *Diagnostic and Statistical Manual of Mental Disorders* (DSM) and most diagnostic manuals give a static concept of the problem, a kind of "photograph" that lists all the essential characteristics of a disorder. However, this classification gives no operative suggestions as to how the problem functions or how it can be solved.

By operative description, we mean a cybernetic-constructivist type of description of the modalities of persistence of the problem, i.e. *how* the problem feeds itself through a complex network of perceptive and reactive retroactions between the subject and his or

---

[4] We should not underestimate the concrete pathologizing power of psycho-pathological and psychiatric labeling (Watzlawick, 1981; Nardone, 1994; Pagliaro, 1995), i.e. the "self-fulfilling prophecy" produced by the diagnosis in the person who receives it and the persons around him. Diagnostic labels, being performative linguistic acts (Austin, 1962), eventually create the reality that they are supposedly describing. Moreover, in the field of eating disorders, we also have the problem of the enormous popular diffusion of psychodiagnostic constructs, which has led to a growing emphasis on these disorders. The great interest and alarm that these disorders produce due to continual publicity have made the symptom an important attention-grabbing vehicle for those who suffer from it.

[5] In the case of phobic-obsessive disorders (agoraphobia, panic attacks, compulsive fixations, and hypochondria), for example, we observed a series of specific and redundant dysfunctional attempted solutions: the tendency to avoid fear-laden situations, constant requests for help and protection from relatives and friends, and attempts to control one's spontaneous physical reactions as well as the surrounding environment. The relationship with self, others and the world of those persons who suffer from these disorders appears to be completely based on the above mentioned mechanisms of perception and reaction.

her personal and interpersonal reality (Nardone and Watzlawick, 1990).

On these premises, we affirm that the only way to know a reality is by intervening on it, because the only epistemological variable that we can control is our strategy, i.e. our "attempted solution". If and when a strategy works, it enables us to understand how the problem persisted and maintained itself. We get to know a problem by introducing change or, as the title of this book suggests, knowing through changing.

This is in line with Lewin's (1951) concepts of change and stasis. He said that in order to understand how a process works one must create a change and observe its variable effects and new dynamics. On this assumption, we have come to know a reality by operating on it, gradually adjusting our interventions by adapting them to the new elements of knowledge that emerged.

The *advanced therapy model* is the final result of such an empirical experimental process, guided by models of mathematics logic, which can be continuously checked and verified, and which furthermore, owing to its formalization, can be replicated and didactically transferred.

Finally, such a model is not only highly effective and efficient but even predictive. This last feature enabled us to develop an artistic practice into advanced technology, without losing its creative aspect, which is necessary for its ongoing innovation process. All this happens while respecting the criterion of scientific rigor.

Obviously, every intervention has to take into account, and should be tailored to, every single patient. As indeed Erickson affirmed, every person possesses unique and unrepeatable features, such as his interaction with himself, others, and the world. Thus, each case always represents something original. Consequently, every human interaction, even the therapeutic one, is unique and unrepeatable, thus the therapist has to adapt his logic and language to the patient's. Only if the therapist manages to understand the underlying logic and use the "language of the patient", he can proceed to "successfully" and thoroughly investigate the problem presented and its specific modality of persistence. Once the peculiarities of the problem persistence are known, he will be able to use the logic of problem solving that seems more suitable. The therapist can now formulate every single maneuver, adapting it to the patient's logic and language. In this way, the therapeutic intervention can truly maintain its capacity to adapt itself to every new person's peculiarities and situation, while remaining rigorous to the intervention's structure.

The strategy is adapted and mould onto the structure of the problem and its persistence, while the therapeutic relationship and the language used need to be specifically tailored to the specific patient. Therefore, even when we adopt a protocol of specific treatment, as for example phobic-obsessive disorders or eating disorders, every maneuver is always different but it always remains the same, because each intervention undergoes changes in its communicative and relational aspect, while it remains the same maneuver at the level of the strategic procedure of problem solving. So we are calling for rigor but not for rigidity.

Chapter 3

Advanced Strategic Therapy Model

"A man is nothing if not the product of his education."
Abbate di Condillac

The advanced strategic therapy model is based primarily on desired objectives. Solution strategies are, therefore, not the logical consequence of a normative theory about sanity or insanity that usually guides interventions, nor are they the logical consequence of a process that defines reality in light of previous knowledge. Solution strategies take into account the characteristics of the problem to be solved and goal to be reached.

The strategic psychotherapist must always have available a series of flexible tactics and tools that can be adjusted to the different patients that he might have to deal with. He does not invent the model of intervention from scratch every time, but is able, based on his experience, to select the strategies he considers most fitting and appropriate for the type of problem at hand and for reaching a specific objective. Moreover, a problem solver gradually corrects and adjusts the model of intervention based on the effects observed during the problem-solving process.

While a model of strategic therapy is rigorous and systematic, it also has the important characteristic of being flexible and self-correcting. It can be modified and adapted throughout its interaction with the reality to which it is applied (Nardone and Watzlawick, 1990; Fiorenza and Nardone, 1995; Watzlawick and Nardone, 1997; Nardone, Verbitz, and Milanese, 1999). This property saves it from rigid, "self-immunizing" positions (Popper, 1972).

The possibility of correcting the intervention based on its observed effects exists at every single phase of the problem-solving process. That means that effectiveness is not measured only between the beginning and the end of the therapy, but is gradually evaluated for each single move and maneuver, so that the model of intervention constantly corrects itself during its application.

Again as in a chess game, every therapy is unique and original. Even though the possible number of moves within a game of chess is limited, the combinations of moves produce an infinite number of possibilities.

To understand the difference between an intervention based on ordinary logic and an intervention that follows strategic logic, we can rely once more on the metaphor of the chess game. Let us imagine that we need to guess which one of the 64 squares of a chessboard a person is thinking about by asking that person the smallest possible number of questions. If we followed ordinary logic, we might have to ask up to 63 questions in order to guess which of the squares the person is thinking about, because we would have to rule out every single square by asking one question at a time. But, if we follow strategic logic, we can guess the square by asking only six questions (see Figures 3.1–3.7 below). Tracing a hypothetical vertical line along the middle of the chessboard, we first ask the other person whether the square he is thinking about is on the left or the right side of the board; we are thus able to rule out 32 squares. Then we trace a horizontal line and ask the person whether the square is on the higher or lower half of the chessboard,

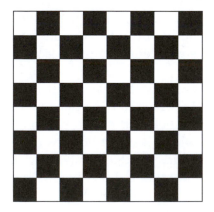

Figure 3.1

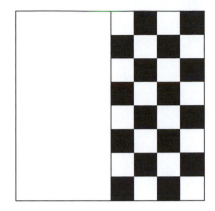

Figure 3.2

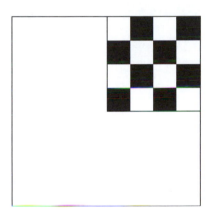

Figure 3.3

Figure 3.4

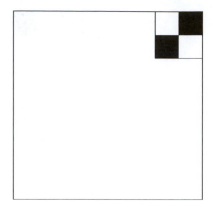

Figure 3.5

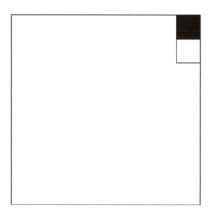

Figure 3.6

Figure 3.7

thus ruling out 16 more squares. By proceeding this way, we eventually divide the chessboard into 8, 4 and finally 2 squares, until we can tell exactly which square the person was thinking about, with only 6 questions.

This is an excellent example of a model of strategic intervention, based on the premise that it is impossible to know *a priori* the right route for reaching an objective. The only way is to start traveling along that route. Therefore, the best we can do is to adapt as functionally as possible to what we perceive.

As a consequence, we can achieve knowledge of how a problematic situation persists only by intervening actively and trying to solve it. The only variable of knowledge that a researcher can control is his own strategy. If the strategy works, it enables the researcher to show the functioning of the reality that is being studied.

In short, strategic logic is based on the construct "knowing a problem by its solutions" (Nardone, 1993); in other words, knowing a reality through the strategies that can change it. Without any claim to *a priori* knowledge of the phenomena at hand, the strategic therapist needs to have some "reducer of complexity" available that will allow him to start working on the reality that needs to be modified and gradually reveal its functioning.

Based on the studies of the Palo Alto School (Watzlawick, Beavin, and Jackson, 1967; Watzlawick, Weakland, and Fisch, 1974; Watzlawick, 1977; Fisch, Weakland, and Segal, 1982), and on twenty years of research in the clinical context (Watzlawick and Nardone, 1997; Nardone, 1996; Nardone and Watzlawick, 2004), such a reducer of complexity has been found in the construct of *attempted solutions*.

When a problem emerges within a certain context (in our case, single patient, couple, or family) there is a tendency to rely on past experience and reapply interventions that have been successful in solving similar problems in the past. If these strategies do not work, rather than applying alternative solutions there is a tendency to apply the initial strategy more vigorously, based on the illusion that doing "more than before" will be more effective. Such attempts to reiterate the same ineffective solution eventually give rise to a complex process of retroactions in which the efforts to achieve change actually keep the problematic situation unchanged. From this point of view, we might say that the "attempted solutions" themselves become the problem (Watzlawick, Weakland, and Fisch, 1974).

It should be clear from our previous arguments that, from the standpoint of change, it is not important to know how a problem was formed in the past, but what maintains it in the present. In order to change a situation, we must stop its persistence. We have no power over a formation process that occurred in the past.

What we have is a "circular causality" between how a problem persists and the ways people try and fail to solve the problem. Therefore, if we wish to make a change, it is important to concentrate on the dysfunctional solutions that are being attempted. If we block or change the recursive dysfunctional solutions, we interrupt the vicious circle that nourishes the persistence of the problem, opening the way to real, alternative change. At that point, change becomes inevitable: the breaking of this equilibrium necessarily leads to the establishment of a new one, based on new perceptions of reality.

This process of change is clearly illustrated by another example from experimental psychology (Orstein, 1986). The reader can easily perform this experiment on himself. Place three buckets in front of you. Fill one with very hot water, one with very cold water, and one with lukewarm water. Now place your right hand in the hot water and your left hand in the cold water. After a few minutes, place both hands in the lukewarm water. The experience will be quite shocking. To the right hand, the water will feel very cold, and to the left it will feel very hot. It is the same brain, but the "right hand does not know what the left hand is doing". The interesting thing here is that, based on the right hand's perception, you would want to add hot water; based on the left hand's perception, you would want to add cold water.

This experiment demonstrates that we construct our behavior based on our perceptions, and that these are based on what we experienced before. An intervention aimed at changing a situation must provide a different experience in the perception of the reality to be changed. This opens the way to different reactions both at the emotional and the behavioral levels.

This process does not merely produce a change of behavior, as some of our critics argue, nor simply a change of emotions. Practical experiences that change a person's perception of reality produce a change at the emotional, cognitive, and behavioral levels.

In the clinical field, this leads to a formulation of therapy that is decidedly different, in theory and application, from traditional formulations. From our perspective, mental disorders are products of a dysfunctional mode of perception and reaction toward reality. It is the subject's recurring attitudes and actions that have constructed this reality. As we have shown, a change in the subject's perceptions will lead to a change in his or her reactions.

The concept of strategic problem solving, which is at the basis of advanced brief strategic therapy, is guided by this apparently simple logic. In clinical practice, this is often expressed by using stratagems, behavioral tricks, beneficial self-deceptions, and forms of refined suggestion in order to guide the subject's experiences in the direction of alternative perceptions of reality. The new, corrective perceptive experiences will lead to a change in the subject's dysfunctional emotional, cognitive, and behavioral tendencies.

The first thing that a strategic therapist needs to do, therefore, is to identify the "attempted solutions" that the system and the persons involved have applied up to that point in their effort to reach a particular objective or to modify a dysfunctional situation. The strategic intervention then proceeds, as quickly and effectively as possible, to interrupt the auto-poetic mechanism that has established itself between attempted solutions and the persistence of a dysfunctional equilibrium.

This type of intervention is made possible by our adoption, in the construction of strategies, of new models of logic that go beyond the Aristotelian logical principles of "true or false" and "noncontradiction". These new models are para-consistent, para-complete and non-aletic logic (da Costa 1989a, 1989b; Grana, 1990; Nardone and Salvini, 1997; Skorjanec, 2000), which have all been developed in the past few decades. Since Kurt Gödel demolished the possibility of a rigorously rational logic in his treatise on "Undecidable Propositions" (1931), mathematical logic has evolved toward the development of these models, which consider *contradiction, self-deception,* and *paradox* as rigorous and predictive procedures in the construction of human beliefs and behavior (Nardone, 1998).

Based on these new types of logic, we can systematically apply non-ordinary logical procedures to construct stratagems capable of leading to objectives or solutions of problems that would seem unreachable and unsolvable if approached through ordinary logic (Watzlawick and Nardone, 1997).

In other words, in cases where ordinary logical procedures (based on the revelations and knowledge of the formation and persistence of the problem with consequent instructions as to how to proceed in order to change) fail, we may turn to alternative logical procedures, appropriate for phenomena that persist on the basis of non-ordinary types of logic. In our view, this applies to most nonlinear phenomena connected with the interactions between the subject and reality, and particularly to cases in which this interaction has led to pathological mental and behavioral expressions.

A concrete example may be useful in clarifying this concept. If we attempt to use reason in convincing an obsessive-compulsive patient to stop his pathological rituals, we will obtain no effect. Instead, we use a stratagem based on the logic of "paradox" and "belief", as in the following prescription: "Every time you enact one of your rituals, you must repeat it five times—exactly five times, no more, no less than five. You can choose to avoid doing it at all, but if you do it once, you must do it for five times, no more and no less than five times."[6] Whether the patient decides to avoid carrying out the ritual or to do it five times, thus rending it a true torture, he will start, in one way or the other, holding control over his compulsion. In both cases, the effect is that the patient will stop enacting his previously compulsive rituals.

---

[6] This prescription, like those that follow, is a techniques that has been formalized in the treatment protocols for phobic and obsessive symptoms (Nardone, 1996).

This prescription employs the same logic as that which underlies the persistence of the pathology, but changes its direction: the force of the symptom is turned against the disorder, with the effect of breaking its perverse balance. The injunction to "ritually" repeat the rituals leads the person to construct different reality from the reality characterized by uncontrollable compulsions. Within this new reality, the person sees the possibility of not performing any rituals, since the ritual is now no longer uncontrollable, but voluntary. We take control of the symptom by constructing another structurally similar symptom, which cancels the former. But, since the latter is a deliberate construction, it can be deliberately refused, as in the ancient Chinese stratagem of "making the enemy go up the attic, and then remove the ladder" (Watzlawick and Nardone, 1997; Nardone, 2003).

These alternative types of logic work as stratagems that induce the persons involved in the problematic reality to change their perceptions and consequently their actions, thus freeing up resources that were, until that moment, imprisoned in the "vicious circle" of interaction between solution attempts and the persistence of the problem.

To conclude this chapter on the theoretical and practical foundations of the strategic approach to psychotherapy, it may be useful to summarize the essential characteristics of this approach:

- The models of intervention are constructed based on objectives rather than on the instructions of a strong *a priori* theory.

- The logic used during the dialogue with the patient and in the construction of strategies is the constitutive deductive, not hypothetical deductive; the solution is thus adapted to the problem, not the problem to the solution.

- Instead of performing interventions based on an investigation of the causes of phenomena, we induce change by applying therapeutic stratagems: it is the fitting solution that explains the problem.

- Constant self-correction is built into the model, which allows us to avoid the continuation of attempted solutions that produce no positive results and often exacerbate the problem that they are meant to resolve.

All these characteristics make our strategic model particularly logical and rigorous as well as flexible and creative. Thanks to these properties, the model has been applied successfully to various contexts—from the clinical to the educational, from interpersonal relationships to the organizational world.

Chapter 4

Clinical Praxis

The Phases of the Therapy

"The strongest proof against any theory is its application."
Karl Kraus

As mentioned in the previous chapters, since its origin, that is the early 1970s, brief strategic-constructivist therapy has undergone constant progressive evolution: from a general model of therapy, to the formulation of specific protocols of treatment for particular pathologies, to the present advanced model.

An essential aspect that renders the advanced model different from its previous historic models is that it goes beyond the idea that systems can reorganize themselves spontaneously and establish a nonpathogenic balance once the old pathologic equilibrium is broken. This idea imposed the interruption of therapy as soon as the unblocking of the disorder was reached. Over fifteen years of clinical experience made us realize that in the majority of the cases, especially when the pathologies persist for years, the spontaneous reorganization of the system, often takes up and re-establishes further pathogenic equilibriums. Therefore, we came to a fundamental understanding, which we applied to the advanced model that a therapeutic phase of consolidation of the unblocking result is necessary in order to constitute a new nonpathogenic equilibrium within the human system, based on its individual features and resources that were unblocked during the preceding therapeutic interventions.

In the traditional models of brief therapy, the therapeutic process subdivided itself into three phases:

Stage 1: Start of the game
Stage 2: Unblocking of the pathology
Stage 3: End of the game

27

The advanced model consists of four phases:

> Stage 1: Start of the game
> Stage 2: Unblocking of the pathology
> Stage 3: Consolidation and reorganization of the rules of the
>   game
> Stage 4: End of the game

It is no coincidence that with such a methodology—which includes a number of specific sessions after the unblocking of the symptomatology—the number of relapses after the end of the therapy has eventually lowered close to zero (Nardone and Watzlawick, 2004).

So, even though in the advanced brief strategic therapy we increased the number of the sessions, this was counterbalanced by the fact that we reached a real therapeutic efficacy. In this way even the historic indictment that brief therapies are superficial interventions or pure symptomatic maquillage is discredited.

Furthermore, the actual unblocking process of symptomatology is also accelerated. In fact, the majority of the cases show a drastic reduction of their invalidating symptoms within the first three sessions and about 60 percent of the cases treated had a significant reduction of symptomatology soon after the first session.

It would be well to point out that the therapeutic process in the present model, besides being characterized by the four phases of problem solving, encompasses a particular form of communication to overcome resistance and activate change, which we refer to as *strategic dialogue*. This instrument renders the strategic interventions even more feasible. We will go into detail in explaining what is the strategic dialogue and how it can be applied in the treatment of different types of pathologies in the coming pages.

However, we will now give a sequential scheme of the four phases of the advanced brief strategic therapy model, which exposes the respective objectives, strategies, and communication style.

Sequential scheme of the advanced model

First Phase: Start of the game

Objectives:
1. Definition of the problem.
2. Identification of the specific form of resistance, suggestive capture of the patient, establishing a trustful collaborative therapeutic relationship.
3. Investigation of the failed "attempted solutions" and breaking the rigid perceptive-reactive system.
4. Agreement on the objectives.
5. First therapeutic maneuvers (intervening, discriminating questioning, paraphrasing, reframing, and prescriptions).

Strategies:
1. Strategic dialogue (intervening, discriminating questions and interrogative paraphrasing).
2. Reframing of the problem persistency.
3. Change-oriented reframing of the perceptive-reactive system and of the failed attempted solutions.
4. Prescriptions.

Communication:
Hypnotic (without trance) suggestive language; injunctive-performative language; illusion of alternatives questioning. Synchronizing technique (using the patient's logic).

Second Phase: Unblocking of the pathology

Objectives:
1. Redefinition of the first change.
2. Stimulation of further progressive change.
3. If no change takes place, use of well-calibrated strategies to stop the failed attempted solutions and start changing the rigid perceptive-reactive system.

Strategies:
1. Use of reframing (cognitive, paradoxical, provocative, inserting doubt).
2. Behavioral prescriptions (direct, indirect, paradoxical).
3. Use of metaphors, anecdotes, stories, aphorisms, explicative redefinitions.
4. Redefinition of the changes obtained.

Communication:
Hypnotic (without trance) suggestive language, injunctive-performative language.

Third Phase: Consolidation and reorganization of the rules of the game

Objectives:
1. Measuring the effects, consolidating results or possibly modifying the strategy.
2. Further progressive changes until the determined objectives are reached.
3. Acquisition of a flexible perception of and reaction to reality.

Strategies:
1. Explicative redefinitions of the changes obtained and further incentives toward personal autonomy.
2. Direct or indirect behavioral perceptions (gradually using a less injunctive style).
3. Reframing.

Communication:
The language gradually becomes less hypnotic and less injunctive to favor, indirectly, personal autonomy.

Fourth Phase: End of the game

Objectives:
1. Complete assumption of personal autonomy.
2. Emphasis on the patient's resources and responsibilities in overcoming and solving the problem.
3. Closure of the intervention which include three successive follow-ups after three months, six months and one year.

Strategies:
Detailed explanation of the work done and clarifications of the process of changed that took place.

Communication:
The language is more indicative, descriptive and colloquial.

In the first and second phases, when the first task of the therapist is that of "capturing" the patient and leading him through "planned casual events" (Watzlawick, 1981) toward the first explosive emotional-corrective experience, the language used should be strongly suggestive-hypnotic and injunctive, otherwise it would be extremely difficult to establish a favorable therapeutic relationship. This is a fundamental element that dictates whether or not the patient will come to observe and adhere to the therapeutic prescriptions. The patient's view of the relationship is crucial in therapy outcome. Patients who perceive themselves as having a "good" therapeutic relationship more likely succeed in achieving the determined goals (Hubble, Duncan, and Miller, 1999). Therapy should be perceived by both therapist and patient as a partnership for change. Duncan, Hubble, and Miller, (1997a) assert that, regardless of how chronic, intractable, or "impossible" a case may appear, if the patient's view of the relationship is favorable, change is more likely to occur.

But, to build a strong relationship with patients, the therapist should be able to determine and take into consideration the patient's type of resistance to change. Different types of resistances require different tactics of communication and stratagems. Extensive research in clinical, managerial, and educative contexts has led to the identification of four different types of resistance to change (Watzlawick, Nardone, 2004).

1. **The collaborative person**: This is a person who from the very beginning is not antagonistic, does not invalidate the process, and is highly motivated to change and holds cognitive resources to overcome his problem. With this type of person, rational, demonstrative communication is the most appropriate. We proceed in Cartesian fashion, discussing the person's perspective on reality in a logical and rational manner until he understands what is dysfunctional about this perspective and thus carries out a conscious change.

    From our experience we have come to understand that this category, unfortunately, comprises a small portion of the people who ask for therapeutic help. When a patient shows a wish to collaborate, the therapist should therefore accept that collaboration, but gradually gauge it to see whether it is supported by facts. However, it is advisable to construct one small initial agreement at a time, then another, then another, until a general agreement is reached.

2. Another category comprises those patients who **would like to collaborate, but are unable to do so.** A large percentage of the patients who seek specialized help hold strong motivation and a great need to change, but are unable to act on this even minimally. This is typical of people who are entrapped in a rigid perception of reality, to the point that at a rational level they understand what they should do in order to change, but are incapable of doing so on a practical level. Usually, these subjects suffer from emotional and behavioral blocks or have strong moral and religious restrictions that keep them from acting in a way that they themselves would consider most functional.

    In such cases, the most effective stratagems turned out to be the indirect maneuvers with strong evocative elements that aim to lead the subject to change without realizing it. In other words, in such cases we use the stratagem of "sailing the seas, keeping it unknown to the skies" (Anonymous, 1990). Following such a maneuver, the process can continue along more Cartesian and rational lines in order to lead the subject to consciously recuperate his resources and skills.

3. **Noncollaborative and openly opposing**: These patients invalidate, protest, and deliberately fail to follow our instructions. The most effective rhetorically persuasive mode is based on using resistance and paradoxical maneuvers. Prescribing resistance to change puts an opposing subject in the paradoxical situation of having to comply with the instructions; in other words, resistance becomes compliance. Even in this case, after obtaining the first changes through a process of influence and persuasion based on paradox, we work on a cognitive re-elaboration of the process of change.

4. The last category embraces those persons who are **unable to deliberately collaborate or oppose themselves**: these are patients whose personal "narration" is foreign to any reasonable sense of reality or whose mental rigidity limits entirely their view of reality.

    In such cases, our intervention has to be well calibrated. We need to assume the patient's non-ordinary logic, codes of language, and attributions, while avoiding any contradiction or belittling the person's constructions. The therapist should follow very cautiously the traces of the person's "story", while changing the course of the person's system of representation without denying its validity. The new direction introduced within the person's mental system will eventually subvert that system. This is just like what happens in physical systems, where entropy with the prospect of evolution leads them toward their self-destruction. In Chinese martial arts, the adversary's own strength is used to bring him to his own defeat; likewise, in therapy, once we have identified the patient's type of resistance we do not fight against it but use it to produce change.

In the third phase when the therapist consolidates the obtained results and guides the patient to acquire confidence in his resources and capabilities, the language used should gradually lessen in suggestiveness, to become a real dialogue. This is a fundamental phase, where the therapist works with the patient to consolidate the achieved results. The therapeutic strategies are focused in maintaining or consolidating the improvements made so far while at the same time they aim to anticipate the challenges that might provoke relapses. In the consolidation phase, change continuous.

In the fourth phase, the last session, the patient and therapist will add a 'frame' to the finished work. The therapist should render the patient participant in what has taken place during the therapy, while emphasizing the latter's resources and responsibilities in overcoming and in solving the problem. It is important that patients come to view change as a result of their efforts and rediscovered resources.

At this stage, patients should come to perceive a relationship between their own efforts and the occurrence of change (Hubble, Duncan, and Miller, 1999). Even if patients attribute change to fate, luck, the expertise of the therapist, or medication, they should be driven to value their irreplaceable involvement in the resulting change and they should be given full responsibility for having been so successful in adopting the stratagems suggested by the therapist in their everyday lives.

During the last session, the therapist and the patient will carry out a final evaluation of the obtained results and of the method used. So, the now ex-patient becomes aware of having been an active subject in the process of change and not a mere object who follows indications. This definitively restores and increments the subject's self-esteem and personal autonomy. People who perceive themselves as capable in influencing and modifying the course of life events cope better and adjust more successfully to life adversities (Taylor, Wayment, and Collins, 1993).

Chapter 5

The First Session

The Strategic Dialogue

"A good start is half of the work."
Aristotle

In more than fifteen years of clinical experience, we have come to understand that concealed behind a request for help by most of the patients who come to therapy is an underlying unvoiced demand, which reads, "Change us without changing us."[7] This double-bind request induced us to search for innovative means of intervention, to use right from the very first session that is free from the usual explanations and rational discourses that our culture and education have accustomed us to use. We understood that we needed to make use of an evocative type of intervention that will lead patients to change their perceptions of reality and overcome their inevitable resistance to change.

In light of this important premise, the latest evolution of advanced brief strategic therapy revolves around the first session and the use of *strategic dialogue*.

In the advanced model, the first session has a fundamental importance because it embraces the first and second stages of the therapeutic process. In other words, during the first session the strategic therapist does not limit his intervention to a mere discrimination or definition of the type of pathology the patient presents, but starts introducing change. This is carried out through the use of a particular type of semistructured interview based on the strategic dialogue.

The strategic dialogue is an intervening and discriminating instrument that involves the language used, the relationship established,

---

[7] According to the brief strategic approach, there are four types of resistance to change (Watzlawick and Nardone, 1997), already described in detail in the previous chapter.

and the logic of the intervention, and is characterized by its all-time orientation toward change.

During these years of clinical-intervention research, we have striven to formulate a particular process of change-oriented questioning that can help us guide a person through a process of learning that will provide him with the impression of having reached certain conclusions by himself, even though those conclusions have actually been subtly induced by the therapist. This is in line with the Spanish Jewish philosopher and poet Solomon Ibn Gabirol's words, "A wise man's question contains half the answer."

Thus, the formulation of this particular model of conducting therapy, i.e. the strategic dialogue, marks the major evolution of the constructivist-strategic approach in recent years.

The model, used in all CTS-affiliated clinics from 1987 to 1995, comprised open-ended questions that followed a more directive manipulative logic of intervention. Resistance to change was overcome with a highly suggestive, hypnotic directive intervention, where the prescription was the apex of the session. With this approach it took two to three sessions to have a more comprehensive description of the perceptive-reactive system, to suggestively capture the patient and overcome resistance, and thus make it to the unblocking prescription.

In the advanced model, all this takes place in the first session, by means of a more indirect and subtle mode of intervention. Even though both models share the same objective, the process of arrival changes.

The strategic dialogue is a therapeutic instrument used for conducting the first session and even subsequent sessions, which is based on a self-deceiving logic.

By adopting the strategic dialogue, the therapist seems to take up a one-down position. He humbly asks a series of seemingly simple questions of the patient, who has the illusion of being the conductor of the dialogue; but, in reality, this method leads the patient toward the discovery of alternatives, useful for solving his problem.

Through experimental empirical research we came to identify certain specific perceptions and consequent reactions, which we call attempted solutions, that keep the subject trapped in a vicious circle with a helpless feeling of having no way out.

These findings helped us devise an instrument that enabled us to understand the patient's system of perception and reaction, and, at the same time, start an *early form of reframing the person's reality.*[8] By asking a series of questions that follow a process of elimination, the therapist comes to an understanding of the patient's representations of reality more quickly and precisely than by asking traditional open questions.

This advanced type of questioning conceals an *illusion of alternatives.*[9] This is one of the most elegant injunctive forms used by Milton Erickson to overcome in a gentle way the patient's resistance to change (Watzlawick, 1990a; Nardone and Watzlawick, 1990; Nardone and Salvini, 2004). In the majority of cases, the application of an illusion of alternatives can be highly efficacious, especially when we need to reframe or prescribe something that we fear will not be easily carried out by the patient. In such cases, the patient is offered two possibilities of choice, the first one designed to be very frightening and impossible for the patient to carry out at this phase of therapy, thus, in contrast, the second choice is seen less threatening and easier to be put into practice. The person will come to accept the second choice, even though he previously considered it to be difficult, because it seems by far better than the first. Thus we create a reality that the person feels forced to commit to. Yet it is the very reality that, if presented as the *only* option, would be considered excessive and so immediately rejected.

---

[8] Reframing is one of the main techniques of persuasive communication, which implies the changing of the perception of a situation by placing it in a different framework that fits just as well, or better, with the "facts" of that concrete situation (Watzlawick, Weakland, and Fisch, 1974). Appropriate forms of reframing allows us to construct invented realities that produce new concrete realities.

[9] Illusion of alternatives is a technique that consists of creating a framework where the individual is presented with a seemingly open choice between two alternatives, but which in reality lead to the same effect—in our case, change.

In the old model, the illusion of alternatives was used in giving the prescription at the end of the session. In the advanced model, aspects of the illusion of alternatives are introduced through out the dialogue with the patient, with the aim of constructing a new prospective that leads to change right from the first session.

Through the use of the strategic dialogue, we can start seeding doubts in the patient regarding his usual attempted solutions and his perception, making the patient come to feel that those attempts usually dictated by a rigid perception—which he had always regarded as being useful means of overcoming his problem—eventually contribute to a worsening of his situation. The intention is to make the patient feel the need to replace an old certainty, an old dysfunctional perception, with a new one. We present a *more functional self-deceiving logic that directs the attempted solutions used by the patient toward their self-annulment.* This procedure is very effective and efficacious because it makes the patient *feel* that this is his discovery.

In order to give the reader a clearer picture of what is a strategic dialogue and how it is conducted, we thought it appropriate to put forward a detailed transcription of a first session of a case of agoraphobia with panic attacks, together with added notes to underline certain significant points.

Therapist: What's the problem that brings you here?

Patient: I suffer of severe panic attacks … for more than ten years … My life has become very limited … I've been to various specialists … but with very poor outcomes … I have great doubts of whether I will ever free myself from this situation. My panic attacks are so severe …

Therapist: OK, but when you have your panic attacks, are you more afraid of dying or of losing control?

Patient: I'm afraid of losing control and go crazy … lose my sanity.

Therapist: OK, but these critical moments, when you feel you're losing control, do they take place in predictable situations or are they absolutely unpredictable and thus can take place anywhere?

Patient: Well, I don't know … However, I tend to have my attacks once I'm away from home … outdoors … I had my panic at the supermarket, on the train, in my car … now I fear all these …

So, from a discriminating, investigative point of view, these two strategic questions reveal that the patient is not afraid of the most archaic fear of human beings: that of dying. He does not suffer a pure phobia but what we came to call phobic-obsessive disorder; he fears losing control and thus engaging himself in uncontrollable acts, as reported by the majority of the cases treated at the CTS in these last ten years (Nardone, 2003). His fear of losing control *makes* him lose control, until he is overwhelmed by panic.

So just as in the chess game, with a couple of strategic questions, we have come to eliminate 50 percent of the possibilities. Furthermore, we now know that the panic attacks take place in situations the patient can predict, can anticipate; therefore, we are not dealing only with panic attacks that take place out of the blue but with the fact that the patient might anticipate when his attacks can take place, so he became phobic of a certain "threatening" situation, which he avoids whenever possible.

Moreover, through the use of strategic dialogue, the patient becomes aware that he is constantly launching a prophecy, which he then helps to fulfill. Slowly and gently, we bring patients to recognize that their anxiety and fear arise at the very thought of having to face a specific situation. From then onwards, there is a build-up of fear and anxiety until they become overwhelmed by panic when they eventually face the threatening situation, which further confirms their prior concern and fear. This is not *explicitly* stated, but we coax the patient to arrive at this conclusion.

This discovery is important both for the therapist and for the patient, who starts to see a much clearer map of his problem; the patient gradually starts to see his reality from a different, more functional standpoint.

After conducting a couple of intervening, discriminating questions, it is fundamental to introduce a short reframing paraphrase or reiteration of the given answer. Thus, after a couple of answers given by the patient, which describe his perception of reality, the therapist needs to sum up and reframe with the use of a para-phrase. Paraphrasing is another fundamental element of the strategic dialogue, because it helps the therapist check with the patient on what has been gathered so far from the questions with an illusion of alternatives, and whether he is on the right track, while starting to introduce small reframing elements.

We start off by saying, "If I'm not misunderstanding you, you're saying that ...?", "If I understood well, otherwise please correct me ..." and then paraphrase what the patient has replied to our intervening, discriminating questions. While paraphrasing, we start introducing reframing elements, but in an interrogative form. We continuously check up on the gathered and reframed informa-tion with the patient. The therapist seems to take up a one-down position, making the patient feel that he—the patient—is conduct-ing the discovery process. This creates a collaborative alliance between the therapist and the patient.

Through these reframing paraphrases, the patient becomes aware of his failed attempted solutions that entrap him into a pathologi-cal vicious circle. This induces him to *feel* the need to change.

Therapist: Please correct me if I'm wrong ... but if I understood well, you suffer of panic attacks that take place in situations that you can predict, situations outdoors, and when you have you panic attack your fear is of losing control, right?

Patient: Yes, that's right.

Therapist: When faced with such predictable situations, you tend to avoid them or you tend to confront them?

Patient: When it's possible I prefer to avoid them, but in certain situations I'm forced to face them: I have to go to work, to do shopping ... It's been more than six years since I last had a hol-iday ... I'm too afraid ...

Therapist: So, if you can't avoid them, what do you do? Do you ask for help or do you face them alone?

Patient: Oh, no, I ask to be accompanied, mostly by my wife ...

These are two crucial questions, since they identify the attempted solution put in action by the patient. The most common attempted solution of obsessive-phobic patients is avoidance. They avoid those situations that they believe might make them lose control. These questions helped us to recognize whether the person is dependent on others or trying to use his own strength when forced to confront his fears. Obviously, each answer orients toward a completely different treatment. So, in this case, the person is dependent on others, especially on his wife. In this case, the treatment should focus on guiding the patient to break free of this dependency and discover his own resources. On the other hand, when a person tends to force himself or tests himself in facing threatening situations, he will be continuously "measuring his own failure" and thus confirming his inability, which further increments his fear. So, in such a case, we help the patient break free of the trap in which he has ensnared himself. We invite him to avoid using this attempted solution that is maintaining and, moreover, worsening the problem.

Therapist: So, if I understood well, please correct me if am wrong … you are a person who suffers of panic attacks that can take place in specific predictable situations, once you're outdoors, which you try to avoid, but when it's not possible you need someone to be near, preferably your wife, who is always ready to intervene in case you lose control, right?

Patient: So true.

So now we—therapist and patient—have a much better picture of how the problem functions. We know where it normally takes place, how the patients feels, how he tries to manage his problem and his limits. When the therapist carries out a precise paraphrasing of the situation described by the patient, the latter feels understood and more confident in the therapist and in the therapy. This helps increment therapy success (Frank, 1973; Hubble, Duncan and Miller, 1999).

Therapist: OK. You tend to speak a lot about your problem or you tend to keep it to yourself?

Patient: We speak quite a lot about my panic attacks ... mostly with my wife, who knew of my problem from the very beginning, before we got married ... However, everyone knows, even the kids, my friends ... They give me advice, they are very patient with me ... Only my workmates are ignorant of this ... I didn't want them to know ...

Therapist: And when you speak about your problem with your wife, friends ... do you feel better or do you feel worse?

Patient: I feel relieved because they can accompany me to places so I can carry out my errands ...

Therapist: So, as soon as you speak about your problem you feel relived, but afterwards, after some time, do you feel better or worse?

Patient: No, after, I feel more frustrated ... before, they used to give me advice on what to do and not to do, but now they don't know what to tell me ... and this is even more frustrating ... I'm also frustrated because I can't do things on my own ... before planning things out I have to see whether someone is available or willing to accompany me ...

So, through these change-oriented questions, the person will come to feel that what he previously thought of as being helpful, in reality is rendering him always more frustrated since this confirms his incapability to overcome his fear (Nardone and Salvini, 2004). He cannot do anything on his own. Once more, we are starting to change the perception and the emotions regarding his usual attempted solutions. This is a central high point of therapy, since patients are normally very reluctant to let go of their usual modalities to overcome their fear.

Therapist: Therefore, if I understood correctly, otherwise please correct me ... you tend to speak a lot about your problem because right there you feel relieved but afterwards you get more frustrated with yourself because you understand, once more, that you're incapable of overcoming it.

Patient: Yes, true.

Therapist: And when you ask for help, to be accompanied, and this person offers you help, do you feel better or do you feel worse?

Patient: I feel better then because I can carry out my errands ... but then I say to myself, "See! You need others, you depend on others." I feel I cannot do it on my own, and that hurts.

Therapist: Ah, so when you ask for help and you get it, at the very moment you feel good because you were saved from a threatening situation ... but afterwards you feel even more incapable, because having help from others means that you're not able to do it on your own, and this makes you feel worse and worse and worse ...

Patient: Yes, that's true. I want to do it on my own but I can't ...

And once more, we are introducing change. Through the use of illusion-of-alternatives questions, followed by reframing paraphrases, we have made the patient *feel and not just understand* that, when he asks for help and receives it, the situation becomes even worse. In therapy, it is important that the patient should *feel* that something has to change, rather than merely understand it (Nardone and Salvini, 2004). We need to change the perception of something and not the cognition, because, if we change the perception, we change the emotive reaction; we then change the behavioral reaction, and, as a final effect, we will change the cognition. What triggers off the change process is our feeling, our perception; all the rest will then follow. One can well understand that one needs to change, but one needs to feel it in order to start doing something about it.

So, going back to our case, our patient now feels that, every time he asks for help and gets it, the problem is made worse. Now the patient is more willing to follow our indications because he feels he has come to this discovery.

Therapist: Allow me to sum up what we've said so far and if I misunderstood anything please do correct me. So, you are a person who suffers from panic attacks, in situations you can predict and thus try to avoid. But, when it's not possible to avoid them, then you ask for help, for support. You tend to speak a lot about this problem, which makes you feel relieved at the moment of disclosure but which afterwards makes you feel worse, because if they listen to you and pity you, that means there's something wrong with you." The same goes for when you ask for help: you feel saved and relieved when you receive help but then, after a while, you feel always more incapable, and the fact that others help you to face certain threatening situation, means that you're not able to do it on your own. And this frustrates you even more.

Patient: That's true.

Therapist: All this makes me recall the words of a famous poet, Fernando Pessoa, who wrote, "I bear the wounds of all my evaded battles."

Patient: That is so true.

Therapist: And I add, "The wounds of the evaded battles seem never to clot, to stop bleeding."

The strategic dialogue induces change by means of an adequate and deliberate use of rhetoric and poetic forms of language such as aphorisms, metaphors, anecdotes, real-life experiences, etc., that creates an overwhelming emotion in the patient. However, it is important to note that, in order to be effective, the chosen rhetoric structure should be tailored to the patient's representative system and be coherent with the therapist's personal style (Nardone and Salvini, 2004). To be able to evoke sensations in a strategic way is in fact a very complex and fine technique that requires great competence in all three spheres of therapy: language, relationship, and strategy.

Once the strategic questions are brought to completion, the therapist proceeds in recapitulating the information gathered, by highlighting the most significant discoveries made, making them merge toward change. Thus, the therapist reassumes in order to redefine (Nardone and Salvini, 2004). To do so we once more turn to a descriptive metaphor, aphorism, or anecdote to portray the presented situation in which the patient can recognize himself and his problem.

We recognize that aphorisms are the most powerful literary communication form, because they are immediate and very evocative. They make the patient feel its effects immediately. Without great efforts it arrives straight to the heart of the patient, producing captivating suggestive effects (Nardone and Salvini, 2004).

The change-oriented questions, the continuous redefinitions, and the final literary recap, together with the overall result of evoking sensations, trigger off a persuasive process through which the patient gradually comes to recognize himself in the new vision suggested by the therapist, while feeling, however, as if he was the one to reach this new vision. Now we can proceed in being more "directive" and thus give prescriptions. The patient will be more willing to accept and follow them.

The harmonious evolution of the strategic dialogue does not only cause the prescriptions to be more acceptable by the patient but they are consequently perceived as some sort of inevitable continuation of the process in progress. In fact, the art of therapy is that of rendering change, not just a desired goal but an inevitable outcome (Nardone and Salvini, 2004).

Therapist: Well, well, well ... I would like you, from now till the next time we meet, to think about what we said today: that every time you speak about your problem you make it worse. I would like to keep in mind that, every time you ask for help and you get it, you will be worsening your problem, even though there and then you feel better. And the same goes for when you avoid doing things. Just as Pessoa did, you will bear the wounds of the evaded battles. But I know that at the moment I cannot ask you to this because you are not able to do so, yet ... Therefore I cannot ask you stop avoiding, but, every time you do so, not only do you maintain the problem but you render it even worse. But I believe I can ask you to stop speaking about your problem because this is easier to do ...

This is a paradoxical prescription. First, we alarm the patient about the prominent danger of his actions, and then we provoke him by telling him that "you are not able to do so, yet." Moreover, if we had to ask the patient directly to stop asking for help, he might have considered it as too demanding and would not have followed our prescription. So, by presenting "the speaking about the problem" as a less difficult task to fulfill, we give the patient the illusion that this requires less effort, even though "to avoid speaking about the problem" eventually eliminates any possibility of "asking for help." We declare that, even though we understand that he is not yet able to prevent himself from asking for help, we are confident that he can at least manage to avoid speaking about the problem. Once more we used an illusion of alternatives to bring the patient to adhere to the prescription. The reader may now see more clearly how the strategic dialogue can gently but efficiently mediate change, by causing the patient to adopt a more functional self-deceiving logic that leads him to accomplish things that he has always regarded as being beyond his capabilities.

Through this complex process of strategic interaction, which follows the lines of Protagoras's sophistic skill[10] and the rhetoric of Blaise Pascal, the strategic therapist leads the person along a path of guided self-discovery, thus incrementing the level of persuasion. Indeed, according to Pascal (1995), "People are generally better persuaded by the reasons which they have themselves discovered than by those which have come into the mind of others."

The strategic dialogue leads to a joint discovery. This helps in establishing a "good" therapeutic relationship and in strengthening extratherapeutic elements that tend to magnify both the efficiency and efficacy of therapy. Research findings show that change is more likely to be long-lasting in patients who attribute their changes to their own efforts (Lambert and Bergin, 1994).

In other words, the strategic dialogue helps us reframe the perceptive-reactive system of the patient through a discovery process, which is made up of what Watzlawick (1981) called "casual

---

[10] Protagoras, one of the most important Sophists together with Gorgias and Antifontes, used a persuasive strategy very similar to the one described here, based on leading the other person, through questions and doubts, to contradict himself and his perception of reality.

planned events," because the events are planned and guided by the intervening, discriminating questions of the therapist but seem so casual to the patient. The strategic dialogue culminates in an explicit agreement when the patient expresses the conclusions that he believes he has reached autonomously.

It is only after this agreement has been established that it becomes possible to go from inductive verbal communication to injunctive verbal communication, i.e. to propose concrete instructions for change. To quote Jullien's extremely valuable essay (1996),

> To manipulate another is to act so that he will want to act, "of his own initiative" and willingly, what I, in fact, wish him to do … He thinks he is deciding on his own will, when it is I who indirectly induce him to it. Since he himself wants it and tends toward it, I do not need to force him, or make an effort to induce him to it.

In these years of active research, we have devised a series of intervening and discriminating questions that conceal an illusion of alternatives, and have started studying and training our students on how to render the strategic dialogue always more efficiently and effectively in relation to specific patients and problematic situations. However, within the same pathology one can find different variants that require different orientation of the dialogue. Our intent is to have guidelines that hold no rigid structure of application but that can guide our investigation/discoveries and our reframing interventions toward change. Our interventions undergo continuous correction throughout the course of the entire session, guided by the patient's frequent confirmations or disconfirmations to our numerous paraphrasing. Therefore we can acclaim that this method is a *continuous self-corrective discovery*.

The strategic dialogue allows us to correct our errors or inaccurate information throughout the discovery process. Thus, it safeguards us therapists from making irremediable mistakes in the discrimination and definition of the problem, and consequently in the treatment entailed. This instrument is undoubtedly of great help for the young therapist, who can feel more confident in his final hypothesis since his partial discoveries are continually checked upon together with the patient, throughout the entire process.

Highlights: The five main components of the strategic dialogue

1. Intervening/discriminating questions that give an illusion of alternatives.

2. Reframing paraphrases allows the patient to confirm or disconfirm the discoveries made while starting to introduce change.

3. Evocation of sensations—use of metaphors, aphorisms, anecdotes, etc. to make the patient come to feel the need to change.

4. Final recap—to reassume so as to redefine.

5. Prescriptions—an inevitable continuation of the shared discovery.

The strategic dialogue has turned the first session into a fundamental part of the advanced brief strategic model, because, besides helping in capturing the patient and identifying the problem with more significant precision, it is a mediator of small yet fundamental change. The strategic dialogue is a vehicle that induces the patient to "feel" the need to change. Thus, we can conclude by saying that the strategic dialogue is the most elegant and evolved persuasive technique that transformed a simple investigative session into an authentic medium of change.

Chapter 6

Advanced Focused Strategies

*"Therapy should always be designed to fit the patient
and not the patient to fit the therapy."*
Milton H. Erickson

Having described the phases and the process of advanced brief strategic therapy and how a first session can be turned into a therapeutic change-oriented process, we established that the best way to enable the reader to have a better understanding of the model and its application to various human problems is to present specific case examples.

Empirical experimental research in the clinical field (Nardone and Watzlawick, 1993; Nardone, Verbitz, and Milanese, 1999) has allowed us to detect a series of specific forms of interaction between the subject and his/her reality, which led to the formulation and maintenance of specific typologies of psychological disorders. This information enabled us to formulate specific protocols for the treatment of the various forms of mental disorders, which to this day have a high, scientifically recognized efficiency and efficacy (Nardone and Watzlawick, 1993; Nardone 1996).

The common dominator of all pathologies, on which we based our specific protocols, is the respective pathology's form of persistence. Paradoxically, the psychological problem is kept alive by the individual's efforts to change and by the efforts of other people who are drawn into the complex cybernetic network of retroactions (Nardone, 1996).

The therapeutic intervention first follows the structure of the persistence, and then reverses its direction by using the same force of the pathology to produce change.

Anxiety and phobic disorders

Fear, panic and phobias are undoubtedly the topics with which we are mostly associated and to which we are attached, given by our long experience in this field of study. Our first work on obsessive-phobic disorders dates back to the late 1980s. The first published research dates back to 1988 (Weakland and Ray, 1995) and it showed that 19.2 percent of the resolved cases took place between the first and the tenth sessions, 61.5 percent were resolved between the tenth and the twentieth sessions, 3 percent were resolved between the twentieth and the thirtieth and 15.3 percent at the thirtieth and the thirty-fourth sessions.

During these last fifteen years, at CTS, we have treated thousands of patients with phobic and obsessive disorders, and this inestimable exposure permitted us to set up a series of specific strategies tailored to the particular type of persistence of each form of recurrent pathology. At present, the efficacy of the advanced treatment model for anxiety, phobia and panic attacks is equivalent to 95 percent (Nardone and Watzlawick, 2004), with a mean efficiency of seven sessions, during which the majority of the cases (81 percent) got unblocked within the fifth session and in 50 percent of these cases there were no traces of the relevant symptoms after the first session.

Panic attacks with agoraphobia

This generalized type of phobic disorder is maintained by the attempted solutions of "avoidance" and "asking for help". Those who suffer from this pathology constantly avoid exposing themselves to some presumed danger, or else require the constant presence and assistance of a person they trust in order to confront them.

Our research and intervention on phobic-obsessive disorders (Nardone, 1996) has shown that, when a subject asks for help and receives it, this attempted solution confirms and nourishes the problem. To interrupt this vicious circle quickly, we have devised a specific, elaborate reframing:

> Well, first of all there's something I want you to think about during the coming week. I want you to think that, each time you ask for help and receive it, you will be receiving, simultaneously, two

messages. The first obvious message is "I love you, help you and protect you". The second message, which is less obvious but stronger and subtler, is "I help you because you can't make it on your own, because you will be sick if left on your own." Please note that I am not asking you to stop asking for help, because I know well that at the moment you are not capable of not asking for help. I am only asking you to think that, every time you ask for help and receive it, you contribute to maintaining and worsening your problems. But please, don't make an effort to avoid asking for help, because you are not yet able *not* to ask for help. Only think that, every time you ask for help and receive it, you are helping make things worse.

Thus, we state that the patient's problem undeniably requires help from other people, but even though this help may at first seem to give beneficial effects, it will eventually lead to a worsening of the disorder. The technique used here is *fear against fear*. The fear of increasing the severity of the problem is much worse than the fears that constantly drive the person to ask for help. Every fear is limited by some greater fear. As the Romans used to say, "*Ubi major minor cessat.*"

So, in this prescription, which is arrived at by means of the already described intervening and discriminating questions, we do not ask the patient directly to stop asking for help. Instead, we use a paradoxical type of communication, which stresses the patient's inability to do without help. In other words, we induce the person to act, without directly asking for action.

This prescription is normally given at the end of the first session, together with the log.[11] By the second session, the patients usually

---

[11] The log is a prescription given in the first session of the treatment of phobic disorders, with the intent of shifting the patient's attention, at the moment of need, from the symptoms onto the performance of the exercise, even though it is presented to the patient as a means of monitoring the panic attack. The prescription reads, "For this task you will be needing a pocket-size notebook on which you will reproduce the scheme I have prepared for you: date and time, place, and persons present, situations and thoughts, symptoms and reactions. This notebook will become your constant companion, which you will need to carry throughout the day; and, every time you feel you are starting to have one of your panic attacks or you feel fear arising, you will immediately draw out your notebook and fill in, date and time, place … OK? However, it is important that you carry out this right then at the moment when you feel you are having your attack, not before, otherwise it will be just a fantasy; nor after, because it will be a memory … we need you to do at the very moment so as to have a sort of an instant photo of the situation. So, even if you have the same sensation a hundred times, for a hundred times you have to draw out your notebook and fill in at the very moment. OK?"

report that they never asked for help during the past week; most times, they even started doing things on their own, realized that nothing bad was happening, and kept at it. They even did things they had been avoiding for a long time, without experiencing any fear.

Usually, we use the same structure of reframing, always in the first stage of therapy, to stop the attempted solutions of avoidance while later we will directly ask the patient to perform specific anti-avoidance prescriptions. When the main attempted solution is that of avoidance, we invite the patient to think that doing so might seem to help at the moment of need, but in reality, this behavior will end up confirming his inability to face the feared situation, which further heightens his fear. So, in such cases, the patient is invited—not imposed upon him—to *avoid* avoiding. Once more, we arrive to this prescription via the use of intervening, discriminating questions and interrogative paraphrasing, as shown in previous pages.

Other patients reveal that they normally tend to avoid fear situations, then they arrive at a point when they feel the need to test themselves by forcing themselves to face planned feared situations, with the purpose of measuring their own failures. Such patients—who, like obstinate warriors persist in the battle using their usual unsuccessful strategy and constantly facing defeat—are induced to understand that their particular attempted solution is, eventually, maintaining and worsening their fear.

As in the "butterfly effect" of Thom's catastrophe theory (1990), a small change sets off a chain of greater changes that eventually lead to the catastrophic event. In the majority of cases, blocking the attempted solution of avoidance, asking for help and of testing oneself, sets off a series of reactions that lead the person to discover that his/her attempted solution lead to the persistence of their pathology. For the first time, patients will experience a panic-free existence.

After the first important change, obviously a whole series of further therapeutic maneuvers are needed in order to reach a definitive solution. The almost magical effect of the reframing does not indicate total recovery from the disorder; however, this first concrete experience starts the process of recovery of the patient's own resources.

But the importance of this specific technique is more easily understood in light of clinical literature that emphasizes the great difficulties encountered in obtaining quick and concrete results in the treatment of agoraphobia and panic-attack syndromes.

The second stage of the therapy deals with the patient's attempts at maintaining control of his or her reactions. To do this, patients tend to avoid even thinking about their fears, but this paradoxically leads them to think about them even more. A specific prescription has been set up to change this perceptive-reactive system.

In the last few minutes of the second session, we assign a new paradoxical prescription:

> Since, in the past week, you have been so successful at fighting your problem, I am now going to give you an assignment that will seem even stranger and even more absurd than the one you have been performing so far. But, as agreed, you must follow it to the letter. I believe that by now I have earned a bit of your trust, right? Now, I assume that you have an alarm clock at home—you know the ones, which have such an obnoxious ring. Well, every day, at an agreed hour, you will take this alarm clock and set it to ring half an hour later. During that half-hour, you will isolate yourself in a room, lie down or sit on an armchair, and during the given time you will force yourself to voluntarily evoke your worst fantasies regarding your problem, think that you are alone, you are feeling panic arising[12] … You will remain in that state for the rest of the half-hour. As soon as the alarm rings, stop, turn it off and discontinue the exercise, stop the thoughts and sensations you have provoked, leave the room, wash your face, and resume your usual daily activities. But for thirty minutes you have to voluntarily …

The prescription follows the Ancient Chinese saying, "To put out the fire, add more wood." Or, as an Islamic maxim reads, "By facing one's fear, one grows to be audacious."

---

[12] The specific content of the prescription should be tailored to each specific situation and person.

This prescription has two kinds of possible effect. The first is: "Doctor, I really wasn't able to become fully absorbed in the situation. I tried, but it all seemed so ridiculous that I wound up laughing. Oddly, instead of making me feel bad, it was quite relaxing" or "I almost fell asleep." The second is: "Doctor, I succeeded so well in doing the assignment that I felt the same sensations as before coming to you. It was very painful; I cried sometimes; then, luckily, the alarm rang and it was all over."

Most patients in both response groups experience no moments of crisis outside the half-hour assignment, while other patients report having had only infrequent episodes of anxiety that were easily brought to rest.

At the next session, whatever the patient's report is regarding the effects of the prescription, we again redefine the situation in terms of positive change. In the case of the first type of response, our redefinition will be as follows:

> As you have had a chance to see, your problem can be alleviated by provoking it voluntarily; it's a paradox, but, you know, sometimes our mind works in paradoxical ways rather than according to common sense. You are starting to learn not to fall into the trap of your disorder and of your "attempted solutions" that complicate your problem instead of resolving them.

The entire session proceeds in the same tone.

With the second type of response, the redefinition is worded as follows:

> Very good. You're learning to modulate and manage your disorder. Just as you can voluntarily provoke the symptoms, you can also limit them and the more you are able to provoke them during the given time, the more you will be able to limit them and make them disappear. The more you are able to provoke them during the half-hour, the better will you succeed in controlling them during the rest of the day.

And so on, for the duration of the session.

Thus, in both cases, our redefinition of the effect of the prescription focuses on reinforcing the patient's awareness and trust in the ongoing change, and on the fact that this person is learning new and efficacious strategies for dealing with possible future fears.

The patient has received unquestionable practical proof that the work undertaken together with the specialist is efficacious. This creates an exceptional collaborative alliance, which helps lead to further progressive changes in the patient's perception of reality.

In the third stage of therapy, the patient will be driven to use this paradoxical reaction directly at the moment of need when the fear is arising. This will make him able to dissolve it. When the subject has gained this ability, we guide him to expose himself to previously avoided feared situations. Most often, patients do that spontaneously, when they have restored trust in their resources. This process, in its completeness, leads to a full recovery from phobic disorders.

When dealing with highly resistant patients, we are bound to use some creative techniques to break their rigid perceptive-reactive system. A particular example of a creative technique, formulated "ad hoc", is the one involving an apple, and is used with a persistent case of agoraphobia with the intent of introducing a concrete experience to overcome a feared-laden situation.[13] The prescription reads,

> Now, on Saturday morning you must take an hour off from work, leave the office, fetch your car, get into your car, but before stepping into the car, you must do a pirouette … you must do it … You come to Arezzo, and find a parking spot in the center. When you get out of the car, you must do another pirouette; then I want you to walk toward the center and precisely toward the market, where you will search for the biggest, reddest, and ripest apple you can find. Only one apple. Then, since I will be here on Saturday morning working like a slave, you will come here, knock on the door, leave the apple for me and go back home. I will be going to work without lunch so you will have to get me something to eat: only one apple—the biggest, the reddest, and ripest one you

---

[13] A full transcription of this case can be found in Nardone (1996).

can find. Put it in a paper bag and leave it here for me. We will meet again at the next appointment. All right?

The following session the patient reported that the mission was accomplished. The entire session was focused on redefining the effects of the prescription, i.e. redefining the corrective emotional experience at a cognitive level. The goal was to enhance the patient's self-confidence and awareness of her resources.

The reader can find out many examples of the techniques devised ad hoc in previous books (Nardone 1996; Nardone and Watzlawick, 1993). However, we have to acknowledge that, since the introduction of the advanced model, these creative techniques are not so much in use in our practice. Resistance to change is now overcome by the use of the strategic dialogue, as mentioned earlier.

Obsessive-compulsive disorders[14]

Another major project carried out at the Centro di Terapia Strategica has been the study of obsessive-compulsive behavior syndrome. We have been studying this highly intimidating disorder and its treatment for more than fifteen years. During this long-term experience, we have treated successfully more than two thousand patients with persistent and complicated obsessions and compulsive rituals. Based on the research-and-intervention method, this study turned out to be a surprisingly good instrument for acquiring operative knowledge about obsessive-compulsive disorders.

The typical perceptive-reactive system of obsessive-compulsive syndromes is maintained by the attempted solutions of avoidance and control of anxiety-laden situations through compulsive repairing or preventive rituals. Repairing rituals are carried out to intervene and repair after a feared event has taken place, so that the patient will not feel in danger, and so it is oriented toward the past. Preventive rituals are focused on anticipating the frightening situation to propitiate the beast or to avoid the worst outcome; therefore it is oriented toward the future. However, recent

---

[14] Adapted from Portelli (2004).

empirical experimental results revealed that there are two variants of preventive rituals: rational-preventive and propitiatory magical-thinking rituals. Rational-preventive rituals are specific actions that arise from the patient's belief that doing so would prevent certain feared situations from happening, for example getting contaminated or infected, losing control, losing body energy, and so forth. The other type of preventive rituals is a form of magical thinking highly linked to fatalistic religious beliefs, superstitious convictions, confidence in extraordinary powers or faith, and so forth.

In all cases, the focus of our first meeting with obsessive-compulsive patients is on creating an atmosphere of acceptance and interpersonal contact in order to acquire power of intervention. Especially with these patients, it is extremely important to support and accept their fixations and their contorted and seemingly illogical rituals. However, even though obsessive-compulsive rituals go beyond the ordinary notion of things, they are not illogical but follow a non-ordinary logic. To be able to change their balance, we need to assume the same non-ordinary logic when devising therapeutic strategies.

A therapist cannot persuade a patient to stop having obsessions or to prevent himself from executing rituals through rationalistic explanation. To do so, the therapist must ask him to do it "better," by suggesting "a more efficacious way" to manage his needs and reach the purpose of the rituals, which is to be able to control his fear. In this way, one enters the patient's perception and, by following the logic underlying the obsessive-compulsive symptomatology and using means of a counter-ritual, the therapist can reorient it toward its self-destruction.

In other words, therapy needs to follow the seemingly crazy logic that underlies the patient's ideas and actions, by declaring to the patient that what he is thinking and doing makes sense. Then the intervention proceeds by giving the patient a specific preset counter-ritual, which is presented in such a way to fit the particular pathological obsessive-compulsive ideas and actions.

For example, if the compulsion is that of checking something over and over again to be sure that it was done correctly, the prescription, using the numerical logic of the pathological control, will be that of making the patient carry out his checking exactly a *prescribed number* of times, every time he feels the need to check.

> From now to the next session, every time you perform a ritual, you must perform it five times—no more and no fewer. You may avoid performing the ritual at all; but, if you do it, you must do it exactly five times, not one more, not one less. You may avoid doing it but if you do it once you must do it five times ...

The logical structure of this ostensibly simple prescription is that of an ancient stratagem: "Lead the enemy up the attic and then remove the ladder." The way the prescription is communicated is very important here. The communication is based on a redundantly repeated, hypnotic linguistic assonance and on a posthypnotic message, expressed in a more marked tone of voice.

The structure of this maneuver is saying that, if you do the ritual once, you have to do it five times. The implication is that the therapists acknowledges the need for the compulsive ritual but at the same time it is he/she who is now in control and is stipulating how many times it has to be performed. Furthermore, the therapist gives the "injunctive" permission to avoid performing the ritual.

In this way, the therapist assumes control of the performance of the ritual. The patient was before forced by his phobia to carry out his rituals, but now he is impelled by the therapy to do so. This means that the patient indirectly acquires the ability to control the symptomatology instead of being controlled by it. If we manage to achieve this by means of the prescription, the patient will start to question his perception, that of being absolutely possessed by his phobic obsession. The fact that he is now capable of controlling the previous pathological actions by following the therapeutic indications means that he could arrive at a point even to stop them. And usually this is what happens. Most often, patients come to the following session declaring they have literally stopped performing their ritual, because to have done so would have meant having to perform it five times. They report that doing their ritual became really boring and they confess that, strangely, they no longer felt the need to perform it to reduce their fear, because the fear never presented itself.

The rationale behind this effect is that of assuming the same logic of the persistent pathology. We have managed to drive its force against itself by means of specifically devised stratagems. In this way, we have made the patient undergo change without any efforts that go against his previous position, by simply utilizing a counter-ritual to break up the "self-feeding dynamic" of the disorder. This technique helps the patient in regaining control over the symptom.

Obsessive-compulsive patients start to perform such rituals so as to feel in control of the feared situation, but paradoxically end up being controlled by the always growing compulsive need to perform them. The attempted solution becomes the problem. The counter-rituals that are tailored to the specific compulsive rituals of the patient steer the force of the symptoms toward self-annulment. To the patient this might appear as some sort of magic, but it is only advanced technology. As Arthur C. Clarke stated in *The Lost Worlds of 2001*, "Any sufficiently advanced technology is indistinguishable from magic."

In the next stage of the protocol, this prescription is maintained and usually the number of repetitions to be performed is increased, while we start to guide the patient to directly confront the previously feared situations.

When the therapy works well, the person lives the concrete experience of freeing himself from both compulsions and phobias. The last stage is devoted to giving the patient a complete explanation of the work done and its process, while acknowledging that the responsibility for the therapeutic success lies in the capabilities and resources of the patient.

During our long experience in trying to put together the best possible treatment for obsessive-compulsive disorders, we have devised many specific counter-rituals prescribed specifically to fit the different typologies of compulsive symptomatology. So we have now, at our disposal, a series of preset specific prescriptions that have proved to be effective with the different forms of obsessive-compulsive disorders.

For example, in the case of ritualistic mental formulas repeated compulsively, we have set up stratagems based on the logic of "killing the snake with its own poison". An exemplary case is that of a young woman who came to our clinic reporting that she had fallen victim to a series of ritualized obsessive thoughts. Several times a day, before and during certain actions, mostly ordinary daily stuff, she felt a compulsion to mentally repeat formulas made up of words or numbers. This slowed down all her activities and had the effect of mentally torturing her, since she considered herself a very rational person and could not accept the idea of being forced to do irrational things.

In cases such as this, we use a prescription that ritualizes the ritual, as described above, following a different type of non-ordinary logic. We take possession of the compulsive symptom by transforming it. The young woman was given the following prescription:

> From this moment until we meet again, every time you feel like repeating one of your formulas, you must repeat them in the opposite way. Say all the repetitions you usually say but do so the other way round. For example, if you feel like repeating the word "man", it becomes "nam". So you will repeat in your mind "nam, nam, nam …" as many times as necessary. If the formula is made up of more words and numbers, the exercise will be more difficult. In any case, you have such a well-trained mind, right?

The following session, the patient reported that the whole thing had been exhausting, but very effective, because after a few days the rituals had diminished, and the day before our session there had been only two episodes, which were immediately inhibited by her performance of the prescribed task. Again, we led the pathology toward its self-destruction.

Another stratagem used with obsessive-compulsive patients who repetitively need to perform religious prayers or other specific rites, is that of creating, on the lines of the patient's rite, another, but one that is more complex and elaborate and, thus, apparently more effective.

Recent empirical experimental findings of CTS demonstrate that preset counter-rituals did not seem to work to the optimum with patients who put into action rational, preventive, propitiatory rituals, with the aim of thoroughly preventing a fear-laden situation. Empirical experimental results cause us to understand that in such cases we have to act on their underlying belief. For example, patients who fear contamination of some sort continuously wash, clean, and sterilize themselves, their houses, and other belongings, to prevent them from being infected or contaminated. But, paradoxically, it is when everything is totally clean, totally sterilized, that fear of contamination starts to grow and thus arises the need to carry out the compulsive rituals. Once more it is the attempted solution that maintains and complicates the situation.

In such cases, by using discriminative intervening questions we should start raising doubts in the patient about whether he should really fear complete cleanliness rather then dirt: "When does the problem eventually raise, when you are dirty or when you are totally clean?" Usually, the first answer is, "When I'm dirty." But when asked, "When do you feel you need to carry out your rituals, when you are a bit dirty or when everything is spotless and you have to protect and safeguard it?", the patient starts having doubts, because he eventually needs to remain clean when everything is spick and span.

"In other words, correct me if I'm wrong, your fear arises mostly when everything is perfectly in order and clean, because it is then that you have to maintain it intact, true? Therefore in reality, you should fear more total cleanliness rather than dirt."

So in this way we start reframing his perception and thus his reaction toward the fear-provoking situation. We have to start introducing the idea that "a small disorder helps maintain order":

> So, from now to the next time we will meet, I would like you to carry out an experiment following the idea that what you should be afraid of is perfect cleanliness. I would like you to carry out this experiment. From now till the next time we meet, you have to deliberately touch with your finger something dirty, something you know is dirty and keep your finger dirty for five minutes, not a minute more, nor a minute less. Once the five minutes have

passed, you are free to wash your finger the way you want. But for five minutes, not a minute more nor a minute less, keep your finger dirty. Five times for five minutes a day, OK?

This prescription follows the idea that, in order to become totally immune and in control of something, one should not avoid or prevent it. On the contrary, one should start to take and endure it in small doses until there comes a day when it will have no effect on one.

We observed that, in the majority of the cases, by simply redefining the situation and setting a series of concrete emotionally corrective experiences, the patient is brought to break free from his attempted solutions and his rigid self-feeding perceptive-reactive system.

The last stage is devoted to guiding the patient and giving him complete explanations of the work done and its process, focusing on attributing the therapy's success to his capacity and resources.

It is of paramount importance to point out that certain patients suffering of obsessive-compulsive disorder hold such bizarre complex rituals that they are often wrongly treated as psychotic patients, as in the case of Roberto, who held a series of preventive and repairing compulsions in order to avoid having his "good" energy sucked away, but who was diagnosed and medically treated as schizophrenic. We chose to discuss and introduce this case in the section related to presumed psychosis because this is an exemplary case of when the diagnosis invents the illness.

Dysmorphophobia

A post-modern disorder that holds the same perceptive-reactive system as all the other phobic-obsessive disorders is dysmorphophobia, i.e. the obsessive fear of one's physical appearance. This disorder is related to our always growing aesthetic sense and to the leaps of progress made by cosmetic surgery during recent decades, in connection with the postmodern notion that we have now advanced so much that we are able to change even the apparently immutable, such as our own physical, genetically determined appearance.

Until twenty years ago, those who longed to better their appearance to become more attractive had to appease themselves by going to the gym or using traditional aesthetic cures, but surely these natural means could not change their physical "flaws". Nowadays, this is possible thanks to cosmetic surgery. In our Westernized culture, both males and females undergo plastic surgery on various parts of their body, confident in bettering their appearances.

Cosmetic surgery is in itself a useful and precious science, but its excessive and improper use can render it decisively harmful and dangerous. Unfortunately, even in this case, what might be useful might become harmful if rigidly repeated. Therefore, when a person becomes obsessed about an aesthetic peculiarity that he refuses to accept, his attention is always focused on this "defect". He lives with this torment throughout the day, which then turns into panic at the sight of a mirror or at an indiscreet glance. Thus the person finds a possible solution and, to try to overcome the problem, puts all his faith in cosmetic surgery.

However, it is necessary to point out that, in the majority of the cases, the aesthetic "defect" is either nonexistent or insignificant. The pathogenic idea of having an unacceptable aesthetic deformation is only a mental fixation, often related to relational problems with others and a profound sense of insecurity. The mind clings to an aesthetic defect to explain the foundations of these problems and holds the illusionary hope that, once this is removed or modified, everything will miraculously fall into place.

Unfortunately, the danger is that this can give rise to a chain of corrective interventions, never resolute, that exacerbates the psychic pathology of the subject. In fact, the person, pleased with the achieved results, can always find something else in his body that can be bettered, thus the patient enters in a seemingly no-way-out trap: he takes up something that gives him the illusion of having control over his physical appearance, but, in reality, it makes him lose all control. One intervention will lead to another, then to another, and so forth. Think of the numerous Elvis Presley or Tom

Cruise lookalikes who roam the globe, products of scalpels and extreme plastic-surgical interventions. Or think of the many people who start off with a simple nose job, then undergo breast enlargement, then decide on an eye-shaping intervention, and end up in a pervasive never-ending game. In such cases, the illusion of a surgical solution leads to more and more interventions, which in turn activate a sort of chain reaction that takes over entirely the subject's thoughts, causing him or her to live in a constant need to sedate the reactions of panic triggered by the idea of having an aesthetic defect.

As in the case of obsessive-compulsive disorders, even in dysmorphophobia, the solution transforms itself into a new problem that requires a new solution, which in turn constructs another problem, and so on. This escalation often leads to real concrete tragic effects, e.g. real deformations, products of a series of aesthetic corrective interventions that might adjust a feature but decompose the overall harmony of the individual. The reader should not overlook the devastating effects of certain unsuccessful aesthetic intervention and of the additional attempts that render even more disastrous the preceding failures.

Another common attempted solution taken up by dysmorphophobics is isolation from social contact, so as to avoid the suffering and the panic crises triggered off by their constant feeling of being observed and judged. Afterwards, they desperately ask for relatives' support for what seems to be for them, the only possible solution to their problem and their sufferings, i.e. plastic surgery. Even though the relatives understand clearly that the problem is psychological and not physical, they end up giving in to this request, because the suffering expressed by the subject seems devastating.

Generally, the dysmorphophobics refuse to undergo psychotherapy, because they are convinced they have a real aesthetic defect and not an erroneous pathogenic perception of themselves. All this makes it difficult to treat this severe pathology and often patients come to therapy only when the disaster has been accomplished.

When they eventually come to therapy, they should not be rationally persuaded into discontinuing this behavior. It will only increase their resistance to therapy. But they should be slowly made to see that what seems to have given them a means of controlling the problem eventually became a bigger problem, which they can no longer control.

To illustrate, let us look at the case of Cinzia. This case of dysmorphophobia was treated by Professor Nardone and it was aired on Italian national TV, during a special edition of the TV program *Medici* (*Doctors*), a series that deals with the latest medical technology. This one featured the idea of prolonged youth. It is a one-session therapy followed by a successive discussion with the patient, which took place in the studios during the program.

Cinzia is a beautiful 23-year-old Mediterranean woman who had already, successfully, undergone breast augmentation before she was referred to our clinic by her plastic surgeon, who refused to carry out a second surgical intervention: upper-lip enhancement.

Therapist: Good morning, Cinzia.

Patient: Good morning.

Therapist: May I call you just Cinzia?

Patient: Why not?

Therapist: Good … tell me, what brought you here?

Patient: My surgeon referred me here, because I asked him to undergo a surgical intervention, on my lips. I want fuller lips, but he does not agree it to be necessary.

Therapist: Mm … So he told you to come and talk to me!

Patient: Yes.

Therapist: OK. Have you undergone other corrective surgical interventions or is it your first time?

Patient: No, I've already undergone another plastic-surgical intervention: I had breast enlargement.

65

Therapist: OK. Did the intervention go well or have you had any problems?

Patient: No, everything went smoothly. I'm happy with the result.

Therapist: OK, so if I understood well, otherwise please do correct me, you underwent a surgical intervention to correct something physical that you didn't like, it was successful and now you wish to correct another thing, which you feel is not really adequate, it is not in the way you want to be.

Patient: Yes, right!

Therapist: The lips.

Patient: Yes, lips.

Therapist: But your surgeon told you, "You don't really need it, so talk to ..."

Patient: Yes.

Therapist: Mm. OK, and that disturbed you? The fact that he said it is not necessary disturbed you, or it reassured you?

Patient: No, let's say that I liked it, because ... from a male point of view ... he told me I was pretty and that it wasn't necessary. But then ... I know what I really like or dislike about myself.

Therapist: OK, but, in your opinion, it is necessary or unnecessary?

Patient: In my opinion, it is necessary.

Therapist: Before the breast enlargement, were you convinced you had to intervene also on the lips or this idea came after the breast enlargement?

Patient: Mmm ... well it was soon after the breast enlargement.

Therapist: So you discovered a flaw in your lips only after have corrected your other defect?

Patient: Yes, that's right.

Therapist: OK … what does this make you think? What does this tells you?

Patient: Nothing! [She smiles and eventually starts laughing.]

Therapist: So you found a defect only after you have corrected a previous one. Does this tell you anything?

Patient: Well, to say the truth … is this … [She smiles once more.]

Therapist: How come you didn't see the defect before, and now you can see it?

Patient: Well, this is a good question?

Therapist: …

Patient: It means that I don't see it any more, because I corrected it and now I look for something else.

Therapist: OK. And do you think that after your lip surgery, you would find something new to correct, or it would be enough, you will feel satisfied?

Patient: I don't know! This is a one-million-dollar question … I don't really know.

Therapist: OK, imagine: you correct your upper lip, you become even more beautiful. It works … Do you think you could see another defect to correct!

Patient: No.

Therapist: Why not?

Patient: Because no.

Therapist: OK, in your opinion a progressing chain of surgical correctives interventions, would make you better or worse?

Patient: Psychologically, they make me feel better, because I'm at peace with myself. And for me this is the most important thing, right? Feeling better about myself. I don't really mind about anything else …

Therapist: OK, so the most important thing to you is correcting defects. Then you feel better about yourself?

Patient: Mind you! No, no.

Therapist: Ah …

Patient: An entire list of things are important to me, one of which is feeling better about myself, looking at myself in the mirror and feeling happy with how I look.

Therapist: OK, but when you surgically correct a defect, you end up noticing another defect and so you proceed to surgically correct it … and then you correct another, then you notice another and so after another …

Patient: This is not necessarily so. Maybe I can stop here, or go on … can't really tell.

Therapist: So it is possible, you can stop here, while you can continue? What can make you stop here?

Patient: To stop discovering other defects. [She smiles.]

Therapist: But at present you see the defect in your lips, don't you?

Patient: Well, yes that's right …!

Therapist: OK, do you know the game of the Chinese boxes? You open a big box and you find a smaller one, than you open the small one and you find an even smaller one, and a then another one even smaller … And so on … I would like you to keep in mind that, after every successful corrective surgical intervention, you'll be overwhelmed by the desire to undergo another one … and then another one … and so on … Simply because the surgical correction truly works and this will make you find a new defect to be corrected and a new one … and so on … In other words, what I mean, is the corrective intervention, that which is making you create new things to be corrected! Do you know Michael Jackson?

Patient: Yes.

Therapist: How many times did he undergo plastic surgery?

Patient: So many times! [She smiles.]

Therapist: Do you remember? He started from the skin, then the nose, then the entire face …

Patient: Let's not exaggerate! That's such an extreme case …!

Therapist: To what extremes has he arrived, no? I mentioned this case, simply to show you how a good solution sometimes can become a problem, if repeated …

Patient: Hmm …!

Therapist: Hmm! My advice is start to thinking that correcting your presumed defects can be helpful to you, for sure, but it can become a problem that creates a new problem that will create a new one … just as in the Chinese boxes game! I used the Michael Jackson image just because it's so strong!

Patient: Yes! That's true!

Therapist: Please allow me to give you some advice, if I may …

Patient: Of course.

Therapist: During the next weeks enjoy looking at yourself in the mirror, five times a day, every three hours for five minutes. Take a pen and paper and note down all the aesthetic defects. Write them down and think how you could correct them. This is a perfect way to avoid the Chinese boxes game, OK?

Patient: OK.

End of the recorded session and back to the studios where there were the presenter of the program, the patient, Professor Nardone and other guests.

Presenter: [to Cinzia] What did you feel on watching the interview you had with the Professor Nardone?

Patient: Well, it impressed me ... it reminded me of a treasured good moment, because this interview was very important for me.

Presenter: A "good moment"?

Patient: Yes, because it blocked me, blocked the things I thought ...

Presenter: Excuse me, but it blocked or unblocked the things you thought?

Patient: No, it blocked the things I thought.

Presenter: You mean your decision?

Patient: Yes, my decision. Yes, the decision to undergo plastic surgery to have fuller lips.

Presenter: Ah ... and why?

Patient: It freed me, unblocked my thoughts. In ten minutes Professor Nardone made me, for the first time, go beyond aesthetic appearance ... what I could wish or not wish. So, for the moment, everything is suspended, because I'm seriously thinking about it. It impressed me.

Presenter: Listen ... So what exactly undermined your previous beliefs?

Patient: The fact that I truly didn't see the problem of my lips before the breast enlargement. For me this wasn't a problem and only after the operation this defect came out.

This is a clear example of how the use of strategic dialogue can change the perceptive-reactive system of a patient in just a single encounter. Through the use of the strategic dialogue, the patient was made to *feel*, and not merely understand (Nardone, Salvini, 2004), that what she was about to embark on was not going to solve the problem. On the contrary, this attempted solution could become a problem that creates a new problem, which will then create a new one and so on, just as in the game of the Chinese boxes! The analogy with the Chinese boxes is a very strong metaphorical image that depicts well the patient's possible entrapment in a vicious circle with progressively worse consequences.

The impact produced by the strategic dialogue used throughout the first session was so immediate and overwhelming that the patient did not need to put in practice the advice given by the therapist, to undergo change. The paradoxical prescription, which we call *aesthetic check-up*, was meant to reinforce the change produced during the session. This prescription was intended to increment the patient's fear of entering into a vicious circle with no ways outs. During the session Cinzia was brought to see that it was the correction of a defect (breast enlargement) that eventually gave rise to another defect (upper lip), which she wanted more than anything else to correct, which thus might reveal another and then another, until she would lose all control. By simply advising her to look out for further beauty flaws and defects, we came to reinforce her presently overwhelming fear: that of entering an endless "game" with no way out. This led to a second-order change[15] (Watzlawick, Weakland, and Fisch, 1974).

Depression

In the last decade, depression has become a fashionable disorder, particularly due to the various debates regarding its biological and environmental causes. A great deal has been written about depression,

---

[15] There are two types of change: first-order change, whereby the system in which the change takes places remains immutable; and second-order change, which, unlike the first, alters the entire system. The latter is referred to as the *change of a change*, because it is more radical and more stable and persists over time. This distinction corresponds to the cybernetic definition given by Ashby (1956).

but we would like to limit our explanations to the successful strategies in the treatment of this pathology.

In the case of depression, the most common attempted solution is expressed in the subject's tendency to complain and play the victim, which is met by an encouraging, consoling, and protective attitude on the part of the subject's family and friends. Therefore at the first stage of the therapy, cases of depression require a specific family-strategic type of intervention, followed by a reframing process of the individual's perceptive-reactive system. We normally call in the whole family and invite them to be participants in the therapy, or, better still, we appoint them co-therapists. This is fundamental for the smooth running of the therapy. Even the language used should employ a collaborative tone. At the end of the session we give the following prescription:

> From now to the next session, you are going to do something very important. Every evening, just before or after dinner, you will all gather together in the living room. Take an alarm clock and set it to ring after half an hour. During the entire thirty minutes all you family members should remain seated in a absolute silence while you [to the patient] will have half an hour to complain as much as you want while they all listen. You will have the opportunity to let them know how unhappy you are, how sad your life is, while they must stay there listening in absolute silence. When the alarm rings, *stop*: the meeting is adjourned to the following evening. You will avoid any reference to the problem throughout the rest of the day: you'll have the evening ritual the day after set aside for this purpose.

We also ask the family members to respect a total silence about the patient's situation until the following evening's session, declining any request by patient in the meantime to be listened to or helped.

In most cases, the family return and say, "Yes, he [or she] complained a lot the first few evenings during the half an hour, but after a while, he didn't have anything left to complain about." Even more interestingly, they usually report that, during the second week, the patient has stopped complaining during the day, and has begun to spend the time doing other things. The depression was all concentrated into the half-hour.

Mostly, we maintain the prescription in the second stage of the therapy but we gradually reduce the duration time. In addition, we use the "as if" technique that reads:

> During the following weeks, I'd like you to ask yourself this question. Every day, in the morning, question yourself: "What would I do differently today as if I no longer had my problem, or as if I had recovered from my problem?" Among all the things that come to your mind, choose the smallest, most minimal but concrete thing and put it into practice. Every day, choose a small but concrete thing as if you had already overcome your problem and voluntarily put it into practice. Every day choose something different.

Patients usually return with a list of little "as if healed" things done. Thus, the depression decreases while the desired things he or she has put into action increase. After some weeks, if the therapy has worked well, the patient will have completely stopped complaining and playing the victim.

The objective of the as-if technique (Watzlawick 1990) is that of introducing some minor changes within the depressed person's daily routine. Even though the change is minimal, it will trigger off an entire chain reaction of changes that will subvert the whole system. This prescription is the exemplary exposition of Thom's theory of the "butterfly effect". If we succeed in making a person change the attitude that makes him construct a dysfunctional reality at least once a day, even in some apparently unrelated context, we will manage to bring about a concrete emotional experience (Alexander and French, 1946) that can be easily incremented by introducing further as-if actions and attitudes, and eventually construct a new functional reality that replaces the previous dysfunctional one.

This prescription is nothing new. Already in the seventeenth century, Blaise Pascal made used of the earliest version we know of the as-if technique to help doubting-Christians to regain their faith. The philosopher suggested, "It does not matter if you now have doubts about God: just go down on your knees, kneel down and pray, use holy water and participate in the sacraments … behave as if you already believed… and you'll see that faith will not linger to be with you."

The small but concrete as-if actions gradually subvert the usual interaction between the subject and his reality, leading the person to really experience something he initially pretended to feel. This takes place through an induced self-deception that changes the direction of the "prophecy", leading the person to experience something different from the usual routine that breaks him free from the old pessimistic perceptive-reactive system.

The combination of the family ritual and the conspiruacy of silence (kept throughout the rest of the day) together with the as-if technique represents a wonderful way in treating most cases of depression, because they jointly work to break the previous vicious circle while concurrently reorienting the patient's resources toward self-healing.

Treatment is somewhat different for those depressive patients who come to therapy on their own behalf. There is a significant percentage of depressed patients who do not involve others in their miseries and try to struggle on their own to overcome this state of helplessness. In such cases we do not need to see the rest of the family but work individually with the patient. Nevertheless, once more our immediate intervention should aim to identify and consequentially block those failing attempted solutions carried out by the patient to overcome this state of depression, and at the same time pinpoint and reinforce functional strategies that can help rescue him or her from this seemingly close-ended labyrinth.

Thus, by the end of the first session, we invite the depressed patients to carry out two main strategies: the *how-to-worsen* and the *miracle* prescriptions.

The how-to-worsen prescription is a problem-oriented strategy aimed at revealing those attempted solutions used by patients, which unfortunately are responsible for maintaining and worsening the problem. The miracle prescription is a solution-oriented strategy aimed at taking the patient beyond the present scenario, to reveal strategies that can help him/her break free from the actual state of being. This prescription aims to provoke stimulating sensations, which will help induce the patient to move toward the desired scenario. Especially with such patients, it is fundamental to work with the their sensations and not the rational, otherwise they will continue stumbling into the usual pitfalls.

The effect of these two prescriptions is usually enough to make the patient undergo an emotionally corrective experience, which unblocks the situation. Patients usually come to therapy astonished by the inexplicable "miraculous" change undergone during the past weeks. Such miraculous change is acknowledged but questioned. Patients are invited to be skeptical about this state of wellbeing and they are paradoxically induced to dedicate thirty minutes daily to thinking about their worst, most pessimistic thoughts. We call this technique "The Half an Hour of Passion," while making an analogue between the patient's sufferings and the passion of Jesus. This technique is an adapted version of the worst fantasy (previously described in the treatment of anxiety and phobic disorders). It has the same logic and objective, which is, "to put out the fire by adding more wood" (see "Panic attacks with agoraphobia" above).

In parallel, we prescribe the as-if technique, described earlier in this chapter, so as to invite the patient to "ride the good wave" hurled by the miracle prescription.

The illustrated techniques were used in the case of Tiziana, a fifty-year-old divorced woman who had been diagnosed as suffering of acute depression.

Co-therapist: What is the problem that brings you to us?

Patient: It's been more than twenty years that I've been suffering from depression. Let's say that it is periodical. Every three years, something happens that triggers it off. Well, I'm deducing this. These are always linked to the love-sphere, something I try to keep under control. For example, last year I had a minor accident, but which was quite bad, where I had my leg plastered. I underwent therapy … Well, I thought, here we go again. I'll get stuck once more in the usual vicious circle, because I can understand how it goes. Now I had this for ages. I was fine until I had a minor sentimental problem … I am quite acquainted with my symptoms. I usually feel my legs and arms aching, and recently I had a terrible painful sensation in my stomach, as if somebody wanted to tear it open. My family doctor—because my neurologist passed away two months ago—prescribed me antidepressant to be taken in the mornings and anxiolytics to be taken in the evenings, for the first fifteen to twenty days.

Co-therapist: To help you rest?

Patient: To help me stay awake. During the first days it's difficult for me to stay awake. Now, my GP gave me this medicine. [She looks in her bag and hands a box to the therapists.] I believe it helps relax the intestinal muscles. It's the only thing that makes this terrible stomach pain go away. It is as if somebody wants to tear it open …

Co-therapist: What about the pain in your legs and arms?

Patient: Well, I couldn't walk …

Co-therapist: And your arms, are you able to move them?

Patient: Absolutely not. Let's say that over the years it strangely became better, probably because I succeeded in managing this depression.

Co-therapist: What do you mean?

Patient: I believe that in some cases I have managed to anticipate it. However, this is my assumption.

Co-therapist: What do you mean by "I have managed to anticipate it"?

Patient: I don't know. I must have anticipated it because nothing happened. When I start to feel like that and can't close an eye, I understand and say to myself …

Co-therapist: … there is something wrong!

Patient: Yes.

Co-therapist: So what did you do?

Patient: Well, I don't know. I reacted against it. I can't understand how certain things happen. I reacted against it because of my job. I have a very stressing but interesting job, it is my drug [smiles] and over these years ...

Therapist: What is your job? We are very curious to know what this drug is!

Patient: [Smiles.] Well, I'm responsible for the Foreign Affairs Department of the Roma Branch of my company [the name of the company was deleted together with any details that might have revealed the identity of the patient] ... My job is very interesting because I'm continuously in direct contact with people ... I like it but it is stressful, it engages me psychologically, because I'm continuously changing, not being myself with others, you know what I mean?

Therapist: Well, you continuously play different roles in order to be able to go along with others.

Patient: True, and this makes me, more often than not, a winner, because I know the person and I manage to understand what to do ... I like the game I managed to establish with people. I feel a winner, but "winner" is not the right word. Let's say I manage to achieve good results, but this is why I'm being paid by my company, no? I feel absorbed by my work. There is a part of me that likes it and another part of me ... However, I can not stay without.

Co-therapist: Sure! But what do you do in times of difficulty?

Patient: I work less, I'm less successful.

Co-therapist: What do you do to overcome your problem, your depression?

Patient: Nothing, nothing.

Co-therapist: What do you mean "nothing"?

Patient: Nothing. For example, yesterday I had a meeting. I stood up and left the room. Once home I lie on my bed, place a nice cushion on my stomach and stay there. Now I can speak about it to my daughters ... I let them know, otherwise they worry about me ... even though I would prefer not to and stay alone in the dark ... I started to feel this way on the seventeenth of February, during the first days I stayed home.

Co-therapist: So you stay home in bed with your windows closed ...

Patient: I would like that, but this is not possible since I have a family.

Co-therapist: You have domestic affairs to manage?

Patient: In the first four or five days I do very little, can't help it, I cry, I'm in total crisis. Moreover, this time round, it happened at the office, so for my colleagues ... let's say for me, these are normal crises but for them ... it is like some sort of panic attack. [Puts her hands around her neck.] I feel I cannot breathe. Who knows what my colleagues thought?

Co-therapist: When you were under medication, how was it? Was it better?

Patient: It got a bit better when I did psychotherapy with him. Then I underwent therapy with a psychologist for approximately six months.

Co-therapist: So you did therapy? What were the results?

Patient: This psychologist was some sort of philosopher who worked with objectives ... our first objective was work, because I had big problems with my superiors in my prior work, but when we started working on the emotional sphere, we came to a halt ... because I had a series of disappointments [says so with great sadness]... in the heart department ... I truly [interrupts the sentence]

Co-therapist: Tell me about it.

Patient: Well, nothing. [With tears in her eyes.] I am not able to handle an intimate relationship with a man. I chose all the wrong men.

Co-therapist: It's as if you can't help choosing men who will end up making you suffer, in one way or another.

Patient: Let's say I had the illusion of having pointed them out … but no. This time I ended up colliding with another of the kind, identical. Well, I was married and then got separated … my husband brought me here. One can say that we have a pseudo-normal life but we have been emotionally apart for three to four years. This person seemed to me … I don't know, I might be attracted by good people but who are a bit over the lines, nuts, not stable, even though I'm in need of strong shoulders …

Co-therapist: So you're in need of strong shoulders but then you end up with men who do not only offer a strong shoulder but who …

Patient: Well, they don't hurt me but they are weak. I understand that they are weak. Because I give the image of being a strong woman and this is my greatest mistake.

Co-therapist: A strong, winning, fully achieved woman.

Patient: Right! So, strong men avoid me, they're afraid of me. Most men are so superficial. Well, most men are, that's what I think. The rest get stuck to me and want to drain my energy, something I no longer want to give away …

Co-therapist: [Nods.] And you continue engaging yourself in this type of relationship, even though they make you suffer.

Patient: Unfortunately so.

Co-therapist: In a game …

Patient: A massacre …

Co-therapist: A massacre—but which, if I understood well, you cannot do without?

Patient: Seems so, but I had enough.

Co-therapist: OK.

Patient: I do not choose well. I'm not able to choose well, damn it! [This is exclaimed with great frustration.] I can't understand why I can't identify them, don't know! They all seem nice people, who make me laugh, be cheerful. You know, this one [referring to her last partner] is suffering from depression too. He is always in bed. We infected one another, you see!

Co-therapist: So please correct me if I'm wrong, you are at present emotionally tied to a man who is also suffering of depression.

Patient: Seems so.

Co-therapist: Do you help one another or does each one of you suffer alone?

Patient: No, I don't want to hear from him.

Co-therapist: When you're depressed you don't keep in touch?

Patient: No. Well this relationship ... we knew each other for three or four years before we got sexually involved. This dates back to last July. He is, professionally, not fulfilled. He took me as an example to follow, but when I reproached him for bad management at work, he ... told me that he never brings anything to completion. I told him so without thinking straight. I was getting even for his couldn't-care-less attitude. What I told him had an aim. I must be sincere and confess that I told him so for a reason, to get even ... but now he isn't well and I'm sorry, but I don't want to hear from him, otherwise I get emotionally involved. I feel sorry and so he drags me along in his problems. Now, I'm sorry to say, I don't feel like worrying about others.

Co-therapist: Have you had other similar relationships?

Patient: Yes, other similar relationships that have lasted even longer. Another relationship, which lasted many years, ended because he was not strong enough to keep up a double relationship. He had a family, but I don't know why he kept seeing me. I guess, I was very important for him, but we drifted apart. He hurted me so much, but he was a positive person …

Co-therapist: And with your husband?

Patient: My husband was the cause. However, my first trauma took place at 24 when my first husband left me. Then I thought that love and marriage were for ever. Then I met my second husband, got pregnant without wanting it. He is the father of my two daughters [points toward the waiting room, where her second husband is waiting], and is very irresponsible. he made me go through a lot, caused me a lot of troubles, especially financially. He stole my money, sold my stuff. Now he lives in my mother's house and I live elsewhere. Things now got a little bit better, because he used to tell me lies, beat me up … I could not cope, he was too violent, yet I'm very attached to him.

Co-therapist: So the pattern repeats itself?

Patient: True, I always approach weak men, infantile, childish men who need to be taken care of—

Therapist: Well! [Interrupts the patient.] While listening to your story, I understood that you have a perfect insight of all that happened to you …

Patient: Yes [smiling].

Therapist: But you can't stop yourself from doing otherwise.

Patient: Damn it, that's what frustrates me most. Don't mind my language. [They all burst into laughter.]

Therapist: We understood perfectly what you mean.

Patient: I get angry because it's beyond me.

Therapist: From all the things you told us, allow me to underline something you say which is so touching. You said, "Strong men don't want me …"

Patient: It's not that they don't want me, it's just they are afraid of me, because I'm quite terrible …

Therapist: Sure, they say, with her [referring to the patient] I'll end up fighting on a daily basis, so it's better if I find someone more acquiescent and I'll be better off. While the weak ones find this force of nature attractive, after some time they discover that you need to be protected and possessed, rather than to protect and possess, and they find you no longer appealing.

Patient: It's not that they are no longer appealing. I would even adapt, but they run away.

Therapist: That's right, because they had an image of you of being strong, reassuring; instead they discover your limits. But there's something that made me reflect, when you said that men don't understand.

Patient: Well, I corrected myself: I said most men.

Therapist: But you're right.

Patient: A bit superficial, no?

Therapist: Well, as long as you continue putting on the mask of a strong woman, so good in playing the role of a brave woman, you will always attract weak men. When you steal their hearts and feel relaxed, you feel you can uncover yourself and remove the mask, and they come face to face with a person they are not attracted to.

Patient: You're right. But with the last one I'd removed the mask immediately. Even though I didn't want to reveal the real me, I ended up spelling it out …

Therapist: But this is an exception to the rule.

Patient: Right.

Therapist: What you told us so far is very indicative: as long as you continue putting on the mask, you will only attract weak men.

Patient: However, it's very difficult to remove it.

Therapist: That is true …

Patient: Even because it is this same mask that helps me be so successful in other spheres of life. I have two daughters. since my husband never brought home a dime, I had to work hard …

Therapist: You were the strong one.

Patient: Always been this way. This is a fact, quite pathological, but I think if I pass away …

Therapist: Please allow me—so you are, in a certain spheres of life, strong. You don't put on a mask, you're effectively so. It's just that, in another sphere, this does not function.

Patient: I'm quite sensible in the heart department.

Therapist: It's just that the same thing doesn't work in other spheres.

Patient: While in other spheres I'm wicked, I'm a dragon, a witch, a lot of men fear me, but what can I do?

Therapist: Another question and then we'll tell you how to proceed. You said that your previous psychologist worked with objectives. Which objectives were reached?

Patient: Well, problems at work, I believe we've solved those … but when we started working on my problem in keeping intimate relationships, well, we came to a halt …

Therapist: Well, I believe we have enough information to understand that we can help you. Our work method is quite specific.

Our therapy is brief. We give ourselves ten sessions. If by the tenth session we don't see results, we interrupt the therapy. If we see we have obtained the predetermined results, we proceed until we come to a solution. If everything runs as usual, by the tenth session your problems will be solved, but this depends on whether you're able to follow us to the letter. We'll see! This is because our work method isn't only based on our encounters or in trying to understand what's happening, because you have already understood everything, no?

Patient: Very so.

Therapist: It's just that you can't do otherwise. Therefore we will give you tasks to follow, tasks that you need to put into practice. Tasks that might seem banal, illogical, stupid, but none of which are harmful, immoral ... which need to be followed to the letter ... In the majority of the cases the problem is solved within ten sessions. We'll see in your case! We have two tasks for you.

Co-therapist: Till now, your objective was to find a solution to your problem. We want to do the very opposite. Every day we want you to ask yourself, "What do I need to do or not do, think or not think, say or not say if I wanted to voluntarily, deliberately worsen my situation?" Every day ask yourself this question ... obviously avoid putting it into practice ...

Patient: OK, but what shall I do when I get anxious about stupid things?

Therapist: Let's go slowly. When the enemy is numerous, we can't confront him at once all together, we need to let it break up and attack it little by little.

Patient: OK, so I need to think what I have to do to worsen my present situation, right?

Therapist: What do you need to do, to voluntarily worsen your situation? Take notes and then bring them along with you the next session. Then we have another task, which might seem bizarre. We want to ... every day when you wake up, while you're getting ready, we want to imagine yourself leaving this room, as you will do today, close the door behind you as you will close the door behind you today, and, when the door closes, *puff!* Just like magic, you're no longer depressed, you're no longer anxious. What would change immediately in your life? What other problems crop up? Imagine yourself leaving this room and, when the door slams closed, *puff!* Just like a miracle, you're no longer overwhelmed by your depression. What changes? What other problems arise? Bring along all the answers. See you in two weeks' time.

Second session

Co-therapist: How are you? You look good!

Patient: Good, very good. I feel more radiant.

Co-therapist: So it is true that physical appearance reflects the heart!

Patient: My stomachaches just disappeared.

Co-therapist: Good, we are so glad!

Patient: It was my worst discomfort.

Co-therapist: When did your stomachache disappear?

Patient: Well, I went back to F— on Sunday. My daughter had a minor accident. She broke her leg while playing volleyball. So due to this, my first day was so and so, but on Monday I woke up so relaxed. It's been a while since I had felt that way. In the morning I usually wake up all uptight, a bit tensed. Since Monday my abs seemed more relaxed, and since then, I have to say, I have been feeling good. Can't explain it! Might be some sort of hypnotic suggestion!

Therapist: Who knows?

Patient: Who knows?

Therapist: If I understood well, you started feeling more relaxed immediately.

Patient: Yes.

Therapist: This state of grace—let's refer to it in this way—now lasts for days!

Patient: Since Monday, after I came to you ... I might have associated, convinced myself ... I don't know! All I know is that since then I feel good.

Therapist: Let's see.

Patient: Let's say I feel quite fine. It's true that a month has passed since my acute phase, but now I feel relaxed more than ever. I face life with less anxiety.

Therapist: How did you carry out the prescriptions given?

Patient: Well I need to read them out. They are quite funny, but I believe you're used to this, no?

Therapist: Yes we are [smiling].

Patient: Well, let's start with the first. What do I have to do to worsen my situation? [She reads out from a long list.] Phone G—, that is my last partner, who is also suffering from depression, or his colleague so as to ask him how he is doing, decide to meet up and then propose solutions to his problems.

Therapist: I see!

Patient: Something I avoided doing. Fix an appointment with my regular clients so as to try to solve their problems, which are also mine. This would create more stress since I'll be having more than an appointment a day. This is highly stressful to me. This is something I stopped doing. I set appointments over longer stretches of time ... didn't feel like going back to the usual hectic rhythm I had until a couple of days before. Make the best of my free time trying to fit in as much as possible, something I always did, I always tried to fit in something to do even in my ten-minute break: visit B—, a friend of mine, so as to set up that famous data, something he has been looking forward to. Phone other friends … things I did not do.

Therapist: Hmm! I see!

Patient: Face J—, my eldest daughter, quite aware that I'm not ready to do so. This won't solve our problems and frequent clashes. Haven't done this yet! Even though, we need to resolve this problem. I'm through with this list. This is the second list. I prepared it in just a day. Want me to read them out too?

Therapist: How did it feel to think about how to worsen your problem? When you came up with things that might worsen your situation what …?

Patient: I thought they were things I wouldn't do, at least at the very moment. In the future? I can't tell! Well, if I fall victim once more of one of these traps …

Therapist: Good. How did you feel doing the morning task?

Patient: The nice one?

Therapist: As if, *puff*!—just like a miracle …

Patient: Well, I already planned to do something that came up after the puff … that is, I will carry it out next week. I thought of taking more care of myself, both physically and mentally … Go to salons and to theatres. Set up a date for my holiday in Prague and that of my daughter in Britain … something I have been postponing for a while. Start a diet and start going to the gym on a regular basis, to the physiotherapist for my backaches. Have a good chat with my boss to clarify my job description and job degree. I've been working now for some years with this company and haven't carried this out yet. Make clear my situation with my daughter, pointing out clearer roles, rules et cetera … I'm through!

Co-therapist: So these will be the things you would do if, *puff*!

Patient: Maybe!

Co-therapist: Therefore all your problems will then disappear?

Patient: Well! [She is not so convinced.]

Co-therapist: You came up with a long interesting list!

Patient: I did the list the day after I came here, but I have to confess that I haven't added anything else since. Yesterday I thought, well, these are the things that I would like to do once I recover but at present I absolutely keep away from doing.

Co-therapist: For now you have to absolutely avoid doing that.

Patient: I shouldn't … even though I'm quite tempted to do so.

Co-therapist: Ah! What does this make you think? The fact that you're quite tempted? Even though we told you that you should not do so because you're not yet ready?

Patient: It's a form of … don't know, weakness! Maybe I would like to do so, even though I'm aware that I shouldn't … but I have to confess that I might do something of the above even though …

Co-therapist: For example, what?

Patient: Phone G—, because I know he isn't well, even though this might hurt me.

Co-therapist: It's an ambivalent feeling: part of you wants to hear from him, another part—

Patient: At a human level … I'm quite curious too, also to see whether I was eventually directly responsible for his depression … This is what I think. Even though he has other underlying problems that are even bigger, I don't consider myself as the queen of his problems. However, I made him confront his responsibilities, as we women normally do, something he's been avoiding all his life.

Co-therapist: And, in one way or another, he was shattered!

Patient: That's what I have been told, even though … I'm quite curious. But I believe I will not contact him because this will surely hurt me … I will do so only when I think that it can be a good thing. Now, it will only drag me into a state of great anxiety.

Co-therapist: And the people around you?

Patient: My family?

Co-therapist: How do your family members live this change in you? Are they aware of it?

Patient: My eldest daughter who studies psychology at university, but not clinical psychology … is contrary to psychotherapy …

Therapist: I believe she would be against all other psychotherapy, except this.

Patient: She's against this too. Because she says that, when a woman has reached her fifties, she can't solve her lifetime of problems in just fifteen days.

Therapist: Ah! Normally our therapy is well received by those who hold a scientific approach.

Patient: Well, you know, Doctor, in most cases when daughters feel responsible, even though she is definitely not responsible for anything, she avoids speaking about this. At home she never speaks about it … I only speak about it with my husband … My youngest daughter knows about it but does not ask questions—she is only fifteen. I said I was coming here but nobody said anything. My daughter did not lend a hand. She says that I tend to pity myself and want others to console and comfort me. I tell her that, if I act in this way, she, who studies this, should console me now and then send me to hell. This is what I told her the other day. In fact during the following days, she was much calmer.

Co-therapist: She calmed down?

Patient: She got more tranquil … We have a very conflicting relationship, also because we have very similar characters.

Therapist: But, if I understood well, she will continue rejecting you, even if you get better, no?

Patient: Surely!

Therapist: She said that you can't get better, recover, in just fifteen days.

Patient: Yes, she says these things don't take place in fifteen days. One needs to do a deeper, slower work, where one can interact in a more confidential way with the therapist, this is what she thinks. She is studying developmental psychology, child psychology. She thinks that after a certain age there is nothing one can do, just die [with irony]!

Therapist: Nowadays, developmental psychology is more oriented toward old age. The psychology of the future is that of the elderly. [Smiles.]

Patient: Surely! That's what I told her!

Therapist: However, our intent isn't to convince your daughter but to help you feel better. Well, if I understood well, you had a sort of magical moment?

Patient: True, I felt an inner calmness, absolute relaxation … it's been a while since I last felt this way … let's say years!

Therapist: Well, well, well!

Patient: Even though here I feel a bit tensed.

Therapist: Well, as we usually say, we have launched a snowball that has started to roll and roll, and it's becoming bigger and bigger … we should let it roll … till it becomes an unstoppable avalanche … by avoiding pushing or even blocking it, otherwise in both cases it will shatter into bits. Therefore, let's leave the snowball we have launched to roll and roll. Thus, we have two other tasks for you, and just like the last time they have different yet converging purposes ... We need you to find half an hour for this prescription, either before lunch or after lunch.

Patient: After lunch is fine.

Therapist: Well, we need half an hour of passion every day from you, just like the passion of Christ.

Patient: The period is right. [This session was held in late March.]

Therapist: Take an alarm clock and set it to ring half an hour later. During this half an hour, isolate yourself, relax ... and for half an hour you need to stay there and voluntarily, deliberately bring to mind your worst thoughts, your worst worries, all the things that made you suffer, all the things that might make you suffer in the future, all the things that frighten you, all the things that make you go into crisis; and let yourself go to these thoughts and to all the things that you feel like doing. If you feel like crying cry; if you feel like screaming scream; if you feel like swearing swear ... until the alarm clock rings, then stop. Leave the room, wash your face and continue your daily routine. OK? But for half an hour you have to stay there and voluntarily bring to mind the worst possible thoughts that might drag you into a state of depression, OK?

Patient: OK!

Therapist: The second task is a totally different thing.

Co-therapist: As you have done in the past weeks [patient says "The miracle fantasy"], yes, the first thing in the morning, we want you to ask yourself this question: "How will I act differently today than usual, as if I no longer had the problem I brought here?" What would I do differently? Among all the things that come to your mind, choose the smallest, most minimal but concrete thing and put it into action ...

Patient: One thing a day.

Therapist: One thing a day, every day, something different. Then bring us the list of all the things you carried out.

Patient: Well, I need to have free time!

Therapist: Well, we are asking from you small things as if the problem was no longer there. But ask yourself this question in the morning, so you can plan it out.

Patient: Right! So I can plan my day better.

Therapist: Fine, see you in two weeks' time.

Tiziana came back to the third session overjoyed by all the small changes she introduced in her daily life. She started taking good care of her health, going to the gym, undergoing physiotherapy, taking long relaxing walks, meeting old friends over a coffee. She also took time off from work to visit Prague. She declared she was much calmer even with her eldest daughter and with her "childish ex-husband." When asked about the "half an hour of passion," she declared that at first she ended up in tears thinking back about all the misfortunes of her life, but after a couple of days she had nothing to think about and that half-hour became her afternoon siesta. Her stomachaches disappeared completely.

The depressed thoughts were concentrated into the "half an hour of passion." Thus following the ancient stratagem, "to put out the fire by adding more wood." The patient was freed from such dispiriting thoughts. This rendered the as-if prescription easier to put into practice.

Even in this case, after such a fundamental "emotionally corrective experience" evoked by creating the problem-oriented task and the solution-oriented prescription, we proceeded in gradually restructuring the perceptive-reactive system of the patient, leading her to construct a new, more functional personal equilibrium.

Eating disorders

The treatment of eating disorder is another important project carried out at the CTS during the last decade. In the course of our experimental empirical study, we observed the existence of several variants among the eating disorders, each pivoting on a specific attempted solution and thus requiring a different protocol of treatment.

For the sake of clarification, we will present some example of protocols. A complete explanation of the empirical experimental research and its findings would have required the presentation of our entire work on eating disorders.[16]

Anorexia nervosa

Anorexia is undoubtedly the most studied eating disorder in scientific literature. During these last ten years, we have come to understand that there are two distinct types of anorexia: *abstinent* and *sacrificial*.

We might say, metaphorically, that abstinent anorexics don a medieval armor that protects them from their extreme sensitivity, but it eventually becomes their prison. Abstinence becomes the *attempted solution* that seems impossible to give up, because, if they took off their armor, they would be unable to manage their emotions.

In the course of our research, we observed how the specific system of perceptions and reactions of abstinent anorexics is characterized by a tendency to avoid eating as well as other enjoyable experiences, because of their fear of losing control. Weight loss becomes a means of anesthetizing emotions. Since abstinent anorexics cannot imagine any personal balance better than their own, they are extremely resistant to change.

---

[16] For more detail regarding the empirical experimental research and its findings see Nardone, Verbitz, and Milanese (1999).

Apart from individual solutions attempted by the abstinent anorexic, the solutions attempted by the system that surrounds her (particularly by her family) are also very important. Family members tend to make all kinds of efforts to help the subject by insisting that she eat, keeping her company, constantly checking on her, etc. Unfortunately, many of these attempted solutions complicate the problem instead of solving it. As Oscar Wilde declares, "All bad art is the result of good intentions" and often with all the good intentions we end up producing the worst consequences.

We normally administer a "mixed strategic and systemic" type of treatment for anorexia. We usually see the whole family in the first session and the young woman alone at the following sessions (we use feminine pronouns because it is mainly women who suffer from this disorder even though research and clinical work reveal that eating disorders are in constant growth even in the male population). If this is not possible, we try to see the family at a later session—at least once in the course of the therapy. As mentioned, anorexia is a disorder that entangles other people, and there are always direct or indirect attempts by the family to make the patient eat. We therefore need to enlist family members as co-therapists. We use different prescriptions in the course of the therapy to guide them, with the goal of blocking all the usual attempted solutions (asking the person to eat, checking on her, etc.).

Sometimes, people suffering from anorexia, like those suffering from vomiting disorders, refuse to go into therapy. In such cases, it is often sufficient to see their parents and persuade them to stop all their attempted solutions.

Most often, after a few sessions with just the family, most young women decide to come into therapy personally because they are irked by the changes in their parents' behavior.

The first meeting with the anorexic patient and/or her family is crucial for a successful therapeutic outcome. If the first meeting is not well conducted, the therapy will very probably be abandoned before it even starts.

Therefore, the initial phase of the therapy requires the "capture" of the patient with the use of suggestion. Right from the very beginning the therapist needs to use some specific maneuvers and communication techniques to establish a verbal and nonverbal alliance with the young woman, to construct a relationship that has the flavor of exclusiveness. It is essential that the therapist learn to use the anorexic patient's particular logic and language.

We completely avoid trying to persuade her to eat. On the contrary, we show respect for her choices and appreciation of her resources. It is likewise necessary to establish an alliance, a trustful relationship, with the family so that all its members will accept and collaborate with the therapist throughout the different stages of therapy.

In the first session, the therapist introduces the following direct therapeutic maneuvers: *nightly letter writing* and *reframing* to stop the family's attempted solutions.

Nightly letter writing

As mentioned, the treatment of *abstinent* anorexics is essentially based on upsetting their emotional anesthesia by establishing a kind of seductive therapeutic alliance with the young woman. At the end of the session, we give her the following prescription:

> From now until the next time we meet again, each night when you go to bed, on your pillow, the last thing you do before going to sleep … you'll need to buy some stationery, preferably a pretty type of letter paper, and write me a letter. There's only one prerequisite: it has to start with "Dear Doctor"—that's me. After that, you can write anything you want, even that I'm mean or stupid … But it must start with "Dear Doctor". When you've finished the letter, sign it, put it in an envelope, seal it, and then bring all your letters to me next time. This will help me understand you and get to know you—better than a lot of talk.

Although we present it as part of a diagnostic investigation, the letter writing is useful for giving the patient–therapist relationship a context of emotional intensity: "The last thing you do on your pillow before you go to sleep …"

The letter written on the pillow evokes exchanges of love letters. Somehow, this seems inconsistent with the words "Dear Doctor." This apparent incongruity fosters a certain level of intimacy while maintaining a "safety limit". It is a classic form of therapeutic double bind (Watzlawick, Beavin, and Jackson, 1967).

What mainly interests us, therefore, is the process of perturbation set off by the letter-writing exercise. This maneuver is also an effective instrument for promoting communication, because the young woman feels free to write things that she would probably find it difficult to say in person.

The nightly letter writing is a first step in establishing both an intensely emotional relationship with the therapist and a process of emotional subversion in the abstinent anorexic. Because of its perturbing effect, this prescription is often enough to break the pathology pattern and to let the patient free from the prison of the abstinent behavior.

At this stage, to ensure a good start, the therapist must therefore intervene directly on the family's communication system by giving prescriptions that put a stop to the most common attempted solutions.

Therefore, the therapist asks the young woman to leave the room and then requests that the family carry out a conspiracy of silence, i.e. that they stop intervening or even mentioning the problem. In giving this prescription, it is very important to avoid any criticism of past actions, or any implication that the family might somehow be guilty. Instead, we must use injunctive language, give positive connotations, and, above all, avoid negative formulations, while praising the parents for having been so good, so patient, and so dedicated in their attempts to help their daughter.

If followed to the letter, this prescription stops completely the usual solutions attempted of the family. This often leads to surprising improvements in the anorexic symptoms. The maneuver is effective because it interrupts a retroactive vicious circle between the family and the young woman, which had been nourishing the problem.

In the second stage of the treatment, having established a relationship of "exclusive alliance" with the patient through the letter writing, we continue our efforts to produce a stirring of emotions by concentrating on the patient's rediscovery of her own femininity. We start by focusing on her ability to be seductive, encouraging her to "toy" with being seductive in her style of dress, mode of speech, hairstyle, etc. Anorexic women tend to enjoy this theatrical aspect very much.

These interventions aim to give the patient some pleasant perceptions and emotions by indirectly bolstering her sense of desirability as a woman so that, as she begins to "feel" something somewhere, she will want to have feelings in other aspects of her life as well. However, we must perform this stimulation without asking too much of her, taking advantage of small things in order to start the process of change.

The young woman needs to feel that she's "working on the problem", but within a margin of safety. It is as if we were teaching her how to jump, but with a parachute! Such small changes tend to have a snowball effect, becoming larger and larger as they roll, until they turn into an avalanche.

During this stage, we continue the nightly letter writing, but gradually tell the young woman to write only if she feels like it. At the same time, we work directly on interpersonal attitudes by applying a particular version of the as-if prescription:

> Every morning, while you wash, get dressed and get ready to go out, I want you to ask yourself the following question: "What would I do differently today if I thought other people considered me desirable?" Among all the things that come to your mind, choose the smallest, tiniest one, and do it. Do one small but concrete thing every day as if you felt desirable. Choose a different thing every day. Next time, bring me a list of the things you did.

The as-if technique (Watzlawick, 1990a) is a positively oriented technique that aims to introduce a minimal change in the person's daily actions. Although minimal, this change can have a butterfly effect (Thom, 1990) analogous to those observed in depressed patients. If we succeed in changing the attitude that has led a person to construct a dysfunctional reality—even just once a day, in a seemingly unimportant context—we produce a *corrective emotional experience*. This experience can easily be expanded by developing further as-if actions and attitudes, until a new, functional reality has been constructed and replaces the previous one. Small but concrete as-if actions gradually overturn the usual interaction between the person and her reality, eventually leading her to experience a real sense of being courted and desired.

As we have seen, we rarely speak directly about what the young woman should eat, or about her problem with food, during the first two stages of treatment (however, this does not mean that we absolutely avoid mentioning it). In the third stage, if necessary, we work directly on the patient's relationship with food, guiding the young woman toward a more correct perception in this context, as we did earlier for other types of feelings. We might, for example, help her recover the pleasures of taste.

Once their symptoms have started improving, anorexic persons often find themselves in the situation of wanting to eat and gain weight, but being unable to do so. The reason is often that they think they are eating an adequate number of calories per day, while they are in fact eating many fewer. These young women have a considerable ability to deceive themselves in their perception of what they eat. It's as if they were wearing deforming lenses that magnify everything. In such cases, we can teach them to weigh "with their eyes" and then with a scale, so that they eventually abandon their deforming lenses for more functional means of perception.

A direct intervention on the anorexic person's relationship with food is also necessary when she has regained some weight and her menstrual cycle has started again, but her relationship with food remains difficult (for example, if she is afraid to sit at the dinner table, or is still eating a very limited amount of food). Since they want to be perfect and in control, these young women assume rigid attitudes toward their diet and do not allow themselves any transgression at all. In such cases, we teach them *the small disorder that keeps order*, with the following reframing:

Behind every boundary, there's a transgression. The more your boundaries are rigid, the more you are tempted to transgress. If, instead, you construct an order that includes disorder, you will no longer feel the need to transgress, because the one *small* disorder saves you from a *huge* disorder and keeps your system balanced and in constant evolution. A small piece of chocolate, a little transgression, means that you don't feel the need to transgress in big matters at other times. One has to allow oneself something. If you allow it, you can do without it; if you don't allow it, it will become irresistible.

The therapist emphasizes the importance of well-organized nutritional habits and decides with the patient what would be a correct and balanced diet for her ("Who knows better than you?"). However, the therapist also introduces the idea that a healthy, balanced diet needs to include a small disorder that keeps the order, because we need a small disorder in order to be orderly.

As you can imagine, this is the best eating attitude not only for anorexic persons but for everyone. Having achieved this goal means having disrupted the anorexic perceptive-reactive system. To confirm this assumption we usually state that, at this stage, the patient includes a small disorder in her diet and she usually establishes intimacy with the other sex without fear. This means recovery, because pleasure is the best antidote for anorexia.

On the other hand, young women who suffer from sacrificial anorexia typically start having these difficulties and develop anorexic symptoms in conjunction with a problematic family situation. Usually, in pathogenic family systems, one member assumes all the weight of the family problem by developing some psychological disorder (Nardone, Verbitz and Milanese, 1999; English version published 2004). This member derives secondary advantages from the disorder because these symptoms allow her to keep the family from shattering, since all other problems are cast aside to deal with the young woman's sufferings.

Therefore, our first intervention with sacrificial anorexics is to give positive connotation to the sacrifice (Selvini Palazzoli 1963; Weakland et al. 1974). The first session is based on congratulating the young woman for making such an enormous sacrifice for the whole family's sake and she is encouraged to continue doing so because this allows the rest of the family to be fine. The reframing goes, "Congratulations! You're making a splendid sacrifice for your family. Thanks to your having the problem, everyone else is in good heath. So please keep it up and try not to change, because, if you do change, everyone will fall to pieces."

Usually, this provocative paradoxical assertion leads to a swift improvement: by prescribing the symptomatic behavior, this will lose its spontaneity.

The positive connotation of the sacrifice has a highly disruptive effect, which is enough to free the young woman from the anorexic symptoms. However, in the majority of cases, sacrificial anorexics hide an abstinent aspect, constructed during the years of sacrification. Through their sacrifices, these young women start isolating themselves from the rest of the world and from social relationships. Thus, in such cases, the treatment continues according to an abstinent anorexic protocol.

Vomiting syndrome/bulimia nervosa

Eating disorders are rapidly evolving toward a kind of "refined" specialization. Young women with bulimic or anorexic tendencies eventually discover that vomiting enables them to control their weight without having to give up the pleasure of eating. Also, by staying just a few kilos above or below their ideal weight, they avoid alarming their families and being pressured to eat normally. Thus, in recent years, we have observed a considerable increase in cases of vomiting syndrome compared with the more "traditional" disorders of anorexia and bulimia.

Although the literature of our field (APA, 1994) still classifies the vomiting disorder as a variant of anorexia and bulimia nervosa, our empirical research has shown that the vomiting disorder is based on a completely different structure and model of perception of reality. Although bulimia (bingeing and gaining weight) and anorexia (abstaining from food in order to lose weight) form the basic matrix of vomiting disorder, the latter, once established, loses all connections with the disorder that initially produced it. In that sense, vomiting disorder is an example of an emerging quality, just as water is an example of an emerging quality of hydrogen and oxygen. Although hydrogen and oxygen are the elements that constitute water, they lose their individual characteristics, since water is something different and more than the sum of its elements.

Undoubtedly, when these persons initially start to binge and vomit, the vomiting represents an attempted solution, a way to lose weight, or avoid gaining weight, while continuing to eat. In other words, it is a way for the person to keep eating without feeling the harmful effects of her relationship with food. Initially, this is an attempted solution that works, but, when the cycle of eating and vomiting is continuously repeated, it becomes an increasingly enjoyable ritual; after a few months, it will have become the young woman's greatest pleasure, and one that she can no longer do without.

Therefore, once the vomiting syndrome has become established, the problem is no longer one of weight control, but one of controlling the compulsion toward pleasure. Eating and vomiting, which started out as an attempted solution with respect to anorexia and bulimia, becomes the problem, and the reason it persists lies in the pleasure that it provides. One of the findings of our research is that the obsessive search for pleasure and strong sensations is a prevalent characteristic of these subjects' perceptive-reactive system.

Vomiting syndrome is structured as a compulsion based on pleasure. It is precisely because this symptom is based on pleasure rather than suffering that it is so very difficult to eliminate.

Our experimental work has led us to distinguish vomiting subjects into three types as well as to set up three different types of treatment. For our purposes here, we will describe only the most relevant.

At the first stage, our main objective is to "capture" the patient, because the young women, whose main attempted solution is vomiting, very often do not collaborate, or may even completely reject the therapy, just like their counterparts, the anorexics. From the beginning of the first session, the therapist must therefore start mirroring the young woman's language and vision of reality, anticipating her feelings, and presenting the eating and vomiting sequence as a metaphorical meeting with her "secret lover":

> Bingeing is the greatest of all pleasures for you, isn't it? It's something extremely difficult to do without, because it's so intensely pleasurable—like having a secret lover. Every time you eat and vomit, it's as if you were meeting a secret lover—very discreet and always available.

We carry on along the same lines for the rest of the session. In most cases, as soon as the therapist succeeds in tuning into the patient's language, the patient will start describing, very clearly and without shame, how her ritual is, indeed, the most enjoyable thing in her existence. Patients sometimes say they feel as if they were possessed by a "charming demon".

If the parents are present, the therapist must try to make them see the situation from the same perspective, and explain that this disorder is based on pleasure, not suffering. The therapist must enable all the persons involved to collaborate in the therapy after explaining what these kinds of symptoms are based on. Toward the end of the session the therapist gives the first prescriptions.

The first one is the *conspiracy of silence*, which is prescribed to the family with the goal of stopping the family's dysfunctional attempted solutions, that is, speaking continously about the problem and trying to convince the young woman to eat.

The second prescription is a special intervention devised specifically for this type of disorder. We give this task either to the patient's mother or to the family member who has been trying without success, to make the young woman eat.

> I'm about to give you a task to be carried out from now until the next time we meet. This task is a bit peculiar. Every morning, I want you to wake up your daughter and ask her, "What would you like to eat and vomit today?" Make her give you the menu. Then go out and buy everything that's on the list, everything she asked for. This should all be separate from your family's daily menu. Place the food well in sight on your living room table, with a note: "Things to eat and vomit for [the patient's name]". No one

else is allowed to touch that food. Only the person who eats and vomits can have it. If your daughter refuses to list the menu, then either buy the foods that were on the previous day's list, or you may choose what to get, because you know what her preferences are. If there are leftovers from the previous day, leave them out on the table. Whatever doesn't get eaten should stay there, together with the food you buy the following days. All right?

By displaying the food and the note in public, we completely reverse the family's previous attempted solution, which consisted of hiding the food, preventing the young woman from eating too much and from vomiting, pretending not to see. We also deprive the ritual of its special characteristic, i.e. its transgressive value. As soon as the patient is free to binge, her perception of the ritual changes completely. By prescribing the transgressive action, we deprive it of its transgressive connotation. When confronted with this prescription, the patient usually gets angry, throws the food away, or eats it a few times and then stops. This is because the emotional experience of eating and vomiting is no longer as enjoyable as before. Moreover, the fact that the food is displayed for all to see, with the note that says, "Things to eat and vomit for …", is usually a strong inhibiting factor.

In the second stage of therapy, we intervene on symptoms compulsion with a prescription-oriented assignment to break its irresistible pleasure-based process.

Since any intervention in the direction of control or repression would only exacerbate the desire to binge and purge, with this type of patient we use a tactic based not on controlling the symptom, but on altering the perception of pleasure that makes the compulsion to binge and purge so irresistible. We prescribe the *interval technique*.

So, are you truly prepared to do everything you can to free yourself from this demon? Well, then, from now until next time we meet, I'm certainly not going to ask you to try not to binge and purge, because you wouldn't be able to do that. You can do so whenever you wish, but you must do it as I tell you. From now until the next session, every time you eat and vomit, you will eat and eat and eat as you love to do. When you have finished eating and get to the moment when you usually need to go and vomit, stop, get an alarm clock, and set it to ring an hour later. So you wait for an hour without eating or drinking anything else. When the alarm bell rings, you run to the toilet and purge, but not a minute before or a minute later...

If we managed to establish a "good" therapeutic relationship and lead a "good" strategic dialogue, we will succeed in making the patient follow this prescription, which will act in interrupting the temporal sequence of the ritual. This alters the ritual's aspect of irresistible pleasure. In fact, this intervention interferes in the pleasurable sequence, which starts off with an exciting fantasy, followed by consummation and then discharge. Since the pleasure lies in eating compulsively and then vomiting immediately afterwards, our insertion of a time interval between the bingeing and the purging deprives the ritual of its intrinsic enjoyment. We thus take control of the symptom through a therapeutic maneuver that follows its structure but inverts its direction, leading it to self-destruct.

If the person accepts to follow this prescription, at the following sessions we increase the interval to about an hour, an hour and a half, two hours, until we reach an interval of three hours or three and a half hours. At that point, usually the subject either stops vomiting or gradually decreases the frequency of the ritual until it stops completely. By altering the spontaneity of the cycle, the interval technique takes away her enjoyment of the liberating act of vomiting, which is usually accompanied by a feeling of almost orgasmic urgency, and by increasing the time interval we make the vomiting more and more difficult and unpleasant. Thus, we transform a rite based on pleasure into an act of self-torture. Moreover, when these women stop vomiting, their relationship with food also becomes normalized: since they are afraid to gain too much weight, they stop consuming enormous quantities. As the symptom decreases, the person's social and interpersonal life starts taking up more space, especially for what concerns her enjoyment of romantic relationships. The third and fourth stages of therapy are the same as those described in the case of anorexia, but it usually works more easily with former vomiting patients.

Binge eating

Binge eating is another example of the specialization in the field of eating disorders, because clinical studies reveal that it does not fit into the other standard categories.

Binge eating is characterized by alternate long periods of abstinence and overcontrolled diets with periods of intensive transgression when they abandon themselves to the pleasure of bingeing (Nardone, Verbitz, and Milanese, 1999).

The attempted solution of keeping control by abstaining from food and by continuously striving to exert self-control is interrupted by a subsequent *loss* of control. The irony is that, the more the person forces herself to control, the more she ends up losing it. Once more, the attempted solution leads to the further complication of the problem.

To free the patient from this vicious circle, we use a reframing maneuver similar to the "fear of help" (Nardone, 1993) previously described in the section about phobic disorders. The strategic therapist induces the patient to fear fasting rather than her bingeing. Using the strategic dialogue, the therapist leads the patient to feel and perceive that, even though fasting might seem the best way to lose weight, in reality when she abstains from eating, she will be preparing her next binge, which makes her lose control and gain even more weight.

The strategic dialogue is used to softly lead the patient to understand what is maintaining and worsening the problem. Through the strategic dialogue and thus the closed-ended-questions which hold an illusion of alternative and the reframing paraphrasing, the patient comes to discover that what she has done so far with the intent to solve her problem, that is fasting or skipping meals, has prolonged her suffering and prepared her next fall to temptation. Trying to stop the binge is useless because at this point it is beyond her control.

The dialogue is led something like this:

Therapist: Is your problem, your incapability to control your eating habits or your obsession to diet?

Patient: Well mainly, I could say my obsession to diet.

Therapist: So if I understood well, you tend to try and diet, and usually you finish bingeing, right?

Patient: Yes, I diet and manage to lose weight… but this doesn't last long. After a while I end up eating more and putting on much more weight.

Therapist: So, your fear is to binge or to diet?

Patient: Bingeing.

Therapist: Are you sure? Previously you have declared that it is the obsession to diet that drives you to binge, so what do you have to fear mostly, dieting or bingeing?

Patient: Bingeing.

Therapist: Yes, this is the real problem. Your attempt is to fight your bingeing habits and not your diet habits but in fact bingeing is triggered off by means of your dieting. If you continue trying to control the bingeing without controlling your dieting, you'll always end up bingeing.

Another attempted solution that needs to be reframed is the misconception that to lose weight one has to eat only and exclusively low-fat health foods. What happens is that these persons start eating tasteless fat-free "foods" that one can withstand for only a couple of days but in the long run will just lead to an increase in the desire to eat the so-called "sinful" foods, with the disastrous result of losing control and bingeing excessively. The secret, which is no secret at all, is to eat only and exclusively what one wants and likes best. Only by doing so can one please oneself and thus not need to binge between meals. Again, it is the attempted solution that is worsening the problem.

Therapist: Do your diets include foods you love best or do you choose the so-called "good foods" for the diet?

Patient: Well, "good healthy foods."

Therapist: Do you choose your food according to its health properties or its taste?

Patient: The healthy properties.

Therapist: Yes, I was sure. So at the moment you force yourself to eat only what is considered to be healthy and "good-for-you," while avoiding all the tasty, mouth-watering foods. So if I understood well, otherwise please do correct me, you eat those foods you *should* eat, and not the food you would truly like to eat?

Patient: Yes, sadly so.

Therapist: It seems that you have rendered something wonderful, such as eating, a true torture with an inevitable consequence, that of fall into temptation and binge. By not allowing yourself your most favorite food, you have rendered these foods irresistible and thus one time or another, you end up losing control and binge on what you have so far so painfully prohibited yourself from.

As the reader could see, the prescription becomes a joint discovery and an inevitable consequence of the dialogue carried out.

Therapist: Thus while keeping in mind what we said so far, I would like you, during the following days, to start thinking about your most favorite food. Every morning bring to mind your favorite food. Ask yourself what would I like to eat today, and proceed to prepare every meal—breakfast, lunch, and dinner—by including your most favorite food without thinking about weight, calories ... Eat only and exclusively your favorite food. Prepare it carefully so as to make it taste good. And eat it enjoying its taste, but eat only three meals a day. You should avoid eating outside these three meals.

As we have seen from these extracts taken from an exemplary case of binge eating, the main intervention of the therapist revolves around the reframing of the attempted solutions that drive the patient to binge. This will consequently lead the person to eat less, eat with more pleasure, while ceasing to regard food as the "greatest" enemy. This will lead the person to maintain a pleasant figure.

For a better understanding of brief strategic therapy in the treatment of this disorder, we are introducing the full transcription of a clinical case. Julie, is a 22-year-old American woman, who has been struggling with her binge-eating behavior and her weight since her early teens. It is interesting to note that, even though this young woman has been suffering from this disorder for nearly ten years and has undergone various specialist interventions before coming to the center, her problem found a resolution in just two sessions. Julie learned about the brief strategic approach and our Center just a couple of weeks before her return to the States, but this did not stop her from undergoing therapy.

First session
Therapist: What is the problem that brings you here?

Patient: Well, some months ago, I think, I started to binge—I've binged a lot before but this time I lost a lot of weight … finals happened so I had to study a lot and I started to binge and it never really stopped. And I found a therapist … but now I'm doing a kind of therapy support by email.

Therapist: Are you only bingeing or also vomiting?

Patient: It depends. Sometimes … I used to binge all the time and vomit afterwards. But now I'm not vomiting anymore.

Therapist: How did you stop vomiting?

Patient: It was tiring; every day even more tiring. My face got huge like a bubble and my roommates were like, "What is wrong with you?"

Therapist: So you had fear of the effects of vomiting and then you stopped. But you haven't stopped binging, have you?

Patient: I can quit binging maybe for one or two weeks. For instance, I quit for a week until yesterday. I didn't binge for six days—that's a long time for me. But during the hardest times at school I start again.

Therapist: Then are you trying to control your eating habits?

Patient: Yes, totally. I email my food sponsor and she gives me a plan for every day.

Therapist: Are you able to respect it?

Patient: For the last six days, I did it. But yesterday I couldn't. I can't go on with these food plans for many days.

Therapist: Are these food plans very restrictive diets or not? How many calories do they allow?

Patient: I used to count calories, do a lot of exercise and even not to eat at all. I was very skinny. But for me in order not to binge I've to let it go. But a nutritionist helped me to make the plans.

Therapist: Let me see if I understand. In case I don't, correct me … Normally, you control your eating habits dieting. You're able to maintain it for some days and then you relax and binge. Is this the usual process?

Patient: Before, when I didn't have a weight sponsor, I tried to maintain diets but I never could. Then I used to binge for three or four days in a row. It made me go crazy. But now, with the sponsor, she emails me my diet and I can follow for the most part.

Therapist: And do you think that your problem is your incapability to control your eating habits or your obsession to diet?

Patient: The whole problem is because of my obsession to diet.

Therapist: You try to diet and usually you finish up bingeing, don't you?

Patient: Or I diet and I'm unhealthy and I lose all the weight.

Therapist: Then your fear is to binge or to diet?

Patient: Both.

Therapist: Are you sure?

Patient: I don't want to diet or binge anymore!

Therapist: But you have said that it's the obsession to diet that drives you to binge, so what should you fear more, dieting or bingeing?

Patient: Bingeing.

Therapist: This is a problem. You're fighting your binging habits and not your diet habits, but the fact is that binging starts by means of dieting. If you're still trying to control the binging without controlling your dieting, you'll always keep generating your binges.

Patient: But I'm eating healthily and I'm not counting calories because a nutritionist, a doctor, told me what I had to eat: proteins, fats and all.

Therapist: I know that very well ... but I disagree, because usually nutritionists indicate a supposed right amount of calories—fat, proteins and all—but they are also advising people to control their diets to build the best diet.

Patient: My food sponsor tells me that she doesn't want me to count whatever: "This is how much protein you can eat, blah, blah ..." The only thing is sitting down three times a day at a table with a fork and a knife. Then, I've absolute freedom ... but I still control.

Therapist: [Laughs.] OK. But, when you diet, do you eat the food you love most or you eat the right food for the diet?

Patient: Well, I love to cook, so I cook food that I love and that is healthy.

Therapist: Do you choose your food for its health properties or the taste that you sense?

Patient: The healthy properties.

Therapist: Yes, I was sure. Your life in relationship with food is to try to control and create the best diet for you. Yet you're eating the food that is an enemy, not a friend ... We have to change that. Do you agree?

Patient: Yes.

Therapist: So, I'm going to indicate to you the strangest thing for ten days or two weeks. I'm asking you to think of your most food. Without thinking about health, just about your favorite food. Can you give me some examples of your favorite food?

Patient: [With great hesitation, the patient takes a long time to answer.] Lobster ... pastries, hmm ... pasta ...

Therapist: And?

Patient: [Again great hesitation, putting great efforts to answer.] Chicken.

Therapist: Uh, chicken ... So, allow me ask you to think every day about your favorite food and to prepare every meal, breakfast, lunch and dinner, with your favorite food without thinking about weight. Your favorite food, your most loved food ... And then, prepare it carefully to make it taste good. And eat them enjoying their taste ... but have only three meals a day.

Patient: But, like what ... like eating pastries?

Therapist: Yes, including pastries. Follow my words, please. If you allow yourself these foods, you will be able to avoid them. If you don't allow yourself to have them, then they will become unavoidable, irresistible.

Patient: But I can't have only one! If I eat one, then I go for ten!

Therapist: Hey! [With an imposing tone that immediately turned soft by the next phrase.] Allow me to try to change this. I know your fear. And that you think that the only way to limit yourself is to control, but your controlling is the best way to make you lose control.

Patient: I don't want to gain any more weight. I've gained twenty-five pounds.

Therapist: OK. Just follow me. [Imposing tone followed by irony.] I hate fat girls. [Patient and therapist both burst into laughter.] My scope is to make you slim and beautiful. So follow me. If you allow yourself to taste the pleasure, you'll be able to avoid it later.

Patient: But there's a lot of things that I like—in reality most of them—that are pretty healthy.

Therapist: If you follow me, you'll discover some really nice realities, OK? That is going to be an experiment, only for two weeks. For two weeks, please.

Patient: [With desperate tone.] But what about if I gain more weight?

Therapist: Follow me, OK? I would like to give you two prescriptions. The first, allow me to repeat it: have your three meals, cook only your favorite food and eat it in the most tasteful way. You have to avoid eating outside these three meals, OK? And the second prescription is, every night when you're in the bed, the last thing you do before you fall asleep, write a letter to me. It should start with "Dear doctor" and you can write everything to me … Write and write and then sign it, put the letter into an envelope and then bring the fourteen letters to me.

Patient: OK.

Second session
Therapist: How are you today?

Patient: [With an expression of content.] I'm good.

Therapist: Yeah? [Touch of irony.]

Patient: I've brought the letters.

Therapist: OK. Give me the letters.

Patient: There is a little mess here …

Therapist: What has been the effect of these?

Patient: I haven't binged for two weeks.

Therapist: Never?

Patient: No.

Therapist: That's astonishing!

Patient: It's pretty good.

Therapist: Very nice! And you didn't binge because you controlled yourself or because the things have gone spontaneously in this way?

Patient: I think it's because I'm not controlling what I'm eating. I don't know, I like the foods I'm eating but I don't like them too much; like I don't want to keep on eating them …

Therapist: OK.

Patient: I'm going to get fatter and I don't want to.

Therapist: But this is the same position of two weeks ago. What's the difference between then and now?

Patient: I don't know. I'm just eating whatever I want.

Therapist: Did you eat everything you wanted? Did you choose only for pleasure as I suggested to you?

Patient: Yeah! I felt less guilty about eating them because I was advised by you, but I don't want to get really fat.

Therapist: But you said to me that you never binged.

Patient: Yeah!

Therapist: But how much did you eat during the meals?

Patient: Sometimes a lot and sometimes a little.

Therapist: What were your sensations when eating only your most preferred foods?

Patient: I've realized that some of the things I thought were my favorite foods in reality are not.

Therapist: So, you discovered something new, didn't you? That some of your preferred food is not so preferred … Unbelievable!

Patient: And once, I started to eat some pastries and I didn't want them anymore. Even the pastry I used to eat all the time when I was bingeing: I had it only once this week!

Therapist: Please allow me to say, if I understood well, when you allowed yourself the taste of the pastries, your supposed favorite food, you discovered they are not actually your favorite. And, thus, you did allow yourself to eat them and you were able to reduce them! It's fantastic, marvelous!

Patient: It's very good. And I thought as well that I didn't feel like bingeing during these weeks. I haven't really wanted to binge.

Last night I went home and I was alone and starving after lunch, but I had only a snack. Usually, a snack it would be, like, uh! [She was about to list the foods she used to eat, when she was intentionally interrupted.]

Therapist: So, let me summarize, did you eat throughout all this time three meals and only these three meals?

Patient: Most of the days. But sometimes I had a snack before meals. Actually no, only last night.

Therapist: Which snacks?

Patient: Yogurt.

Therapist: Yogurt is one of your most foods?

Patient: Yes.

Therapist: OK. Why not? I'm curious to investigate your sensations in allowing yourself to taste your favorite foods.

Patient: At the beginning, I didn't know what to eat. I went around with my roommate to spot what she bought and I thought it looked good. In two years I haven't enjoyed any food; I don't remember having bought any food that I like. And even when I was buying food I was looking at the labels to look for the calories.

Therapist: I know you do that well. It's the classic pattern of interaction that bingeing women like you have with food: so as to control everything related to food.

Patient: It was hard not to do that. I went to the market instead of the supermarket, just to buy food without labels.

Therapist: Oh, without labels!

Patient: Yes, because I want to stop. I hate my body right now.

Therapist: If I understood well, otherwise do correct me, you have been eating only for pleasure during the meals, except one time when you ate a yogurt before going to sleep, but never binged.

Patient: But last night, at dinner, they bought these potato things and there was a big plate for all the table and then I tried one and I just kept eating them. I didn't like them that much.

Therapist: Let me ask you, what has changed in your relationship with food during this week?

Patient: I can have whatever I want.

Therapist: Ah, you can have whatever you want and you can avoid. That's a nice discovery! Because, as I said to you in the past sessions, the more you try to control yourself, the more you lose control. It's always the same with pleasure. With everything we feel pleasurable about in our life, the more we try to control, the more we lose control of it. So, you've made a real discovery. You can change your perception. You can start to interact with food in a different way and allow yourself to taste the tastiest things, and since you allow yourself these foods, you can then choose to refuse them but if you do not allow yourself these foods, they will become irresistible.

Patient: But I'm going to gain so much more weight!

Therapist: We'll look into that. Let me say to you it's possible that you will discover some other interesting things, but now I'm not going to explain it to you. You'll discover new things if you allow yourself the most tasty things. You'll also be able to avoid bingeing. So what about the letters?

Patient: I didn't know what you want me to write so I just wrote letters. I wrote about—when I was going to write about the foods I love—the foods I hate. But without thinking, not purposely.

Therapist: OK. So let me suggest the second stage of your work. And let me say to you that I'm really impressed with your ability to follow the work. You're really a smart person. You've to continue like this, looking only for your most preferred food. Besides the three meals, if you want to, you can sometimes have a yogurt. But at breakfast, lunch, and dinner, you have to choose your most preferred food, as you have done.

Patient: But what about if I gain weight?

Therapist: Please, go on and you will discover some other nice things. Trust me.

Patient: What about working out, going to the gym?

Therapist: Yes, you can work out, but don't overdo it. The best way to keep yourself fit is to do half an hour of aerobic exercise followed by fifteen minutes of stretching a day. This is the best way. No more.

Patient: No more?

Therapist: No more, because more will become dangerous, because it pushes you to feel more hungry.

Patient: How many days a week?

Therapist: Seven days for half an hour and fifteen minutes.

Patient: For me seven days is too much.

Therapist: [Laughing.] Just half an hour of jogging and fifteen minutes of stretching. This is the best exercise for a diet, but the best diet is eating your favorite food during the three meals, because you have discovered that in this way you can avoid bingeing. In this way, you're not nervous and hungry to a point where you feel forced to eat. The letters will now be an option, not an obligation. You can decide to write them or not. The really new task is a question you have to ask yourself every morning: "What will I do differently today—as if my problem had vanished completely?" Ask yourself this and then choose the smallest thing among the things you have thought about. Choose the smallest thing you would do if your problem were completely solved and put it into action.

Patient: Interesting.

Since Julie had to return to the States, we had arranged to have follow-ups via telephone. We had three follow-up calls from Julie over a period of six months during which she declared that she had stopped completely her bingeing while she continued eating only the food she liked best, and to her surprise she had also managed to lose four kilos, which she managed to keep thanks to her new lifestyle (three daily meals and regular exercising). Furthermore, the as-if technique triggered off an overwhelming change in her social life and physical appearance. She started paying more attention to herself, her needs, and her pastimes.

Blocked-performance pathologies

With blocked-performance pathologies, we refer to all those actions that are brought to a halt due to the subject's over anxiety and fear of failing. These include stage-fright, fear of speaking in public, of blanking out at exams or interviews, of sexual and athletic fiascos, and blockage of other performances, where the individual feels that he has to prove himself.

In our experience most of blocked-performance therapy is really similar to that used for obsessive and phobic disorders. In fact, the main attempted solution maintaining the problem is to try to maintain control, which ironically drives to *loss* of control. As you might realize, it is the same typical attempted solution as that of the panic syndrome, therefore the therapeutic strategy used is that of training the patient to voluntarily lose control so as, paradoxically, to be able to maintain it. In other words, we reverse the patient's perceptive-reactive system on itself to reach self-annulment.

In practice, we use the progressive prescriptions of the half an hour of worst fantasy, followed by the use of the same, by-now-learned technique, when coming to face the fearing and blocking situation, to paradoxically anticipate and manage it. Usually, this strategy enables patients to overcome their problem and makes them able to mobilize their previously blocked personal resources.

This was the case of a fifty-year-old marketing manager of a prominent Italian company. He phoned our Center to request an urgent appointment. We fixed the appointment for the day after, when he confessed that he was overwhelmed by a problem that was "threatening to destroy" his professional life. In the past few months, he had become terrified to speak in public. Thus, during these months, he had invented all sort of excuses to avoid doing so. Until then, he had confidently delivered speeches at conventions in front of hundreds of colleagues. For several years, he had also carried out training courses to numerous top managers. That is why he could not come to terms with his present fear. He was quite desperate because a week or so after our encounter he had to put forward, during a convention, the company's marketing plan, and this time there were no ways out.

When asked about his greatest fear, he replied that he feared that his mind would become a blank while he was presenting his speeches in front of the company's demanding executives. This would create great embarrassment to him and his company.

The problem had first appeared during one of the many congresses at which he was invited to speak, where he had witnessed a colleague undergo a severe anxiety crisis. Since then, he had become terrified that the same thing could happen to him. Just the thought of having to stand in front of his colleagues made him feel sick.

So, during these months, he had planned his work schedule in order to avoid having to speak in public, but without letting anybody notice his distress. He had involved himself in various projects, so to distract himself from his fear.

Having gathered all the required information, we gave this patient the following prescription:

> From now till the day of the convention, we would like you to carry out this task. Every day, during your lunch break, you will take an alarm clock or you can use your mobile phone and set it to ring half an hour later. During this half-hour, you will isolate yourself in your office, lie back on a comfy chair, and during the given time you will force yourself to evoke your worst fantasies, imagine

yourself in front of hundreds of demanding managers who have no time to lose, imagine that you have to start your speech but you cannot remember the starting line, what to say. Your mind goes blank while everyone is looking at you, waiting for your words, you start feeling panicky. You start to sweat[17] … if you feel you need to scream, go ahead and scream, but for the half-hour you have to force yourself to bring to mind your worst fantasies. As soon as the alarm rings, stop, turn it off and discontinue the exercise, stop the thoughts and sensations you have provoked, leave the office, wash your face, and then resume your office activities.

Thus, the patient is invited to carry out this assignment on a daily basis until the big day.

On the day of the presentation, we would like you to do the following. In the hour before your speech, try to bring to mind all your worst possible fantasies; no need to isolate yourself, do it mentally. Concentrate all your anxiety in that hour before the speech. That way, you will feel much less anxious afterwards. When it's time for you to speak, if you feel you are fine, go ahead and give your speech. If you still feel tension rising, take your place and start by saying, "Dear colleagues, I'm going to ask you in advance to please excuse me if I start to blush, sweat, or lose track of my argument but I have not been feeling very well lately." Then present your report.

The man reacted by saying that our last request would have made him feel embarrassed in front of his colleagues. Our reply was that if he followed us to the letter he might have a pleasant surprise, but that we did not want to reveal it in advance.

We saw him after two weeks, but he had called a few days before our session to thank us and let us know that things had gone very well.

On our second meeting, he reported that he had followed our instructions to the letter. He proclaimed that every day he had invoked his "ghosts"—he truly managed to think about a variety of things that might have gone wrong while delivering his

---

[17] The specific content of the prescription should be tailored to each specific situation and person.

speech—and yet, surprisingly, every day he felt less anxious and more confident in succeeding. On the day of the speech, during the last hour he recited his speech mentally while trying to provoke himself to fear, but he felt so tranquil that, once he took his place, he did not need to claim he was unwell. His speech went smoothly, as did a board meeting that followed some days later.

So, in this case, one of the most ineffective attempted solutions was that of trying to keep control over the situation by avoiding public speeches and avoiding thinking about what might happened with the intention of limiting his fear. But trying not to think about something is also the best way to think even more about it. So, in such cases as blocking of performance, we proceed to prescribe a daily space and time, precisely planned, with a beginning and an end, in which the patient voluntarily concentrates all his worst fantasies. This will help direct and release his anxiety and fear of drying up in public.

As we saw earlier when we illustrated the treatment for phobic-obsessive disorders, the prescription succeeds in making the patient feel very miserable during the assigned time but relieves his anxiety during the rest of the day, and, in the case of blocked performance, this will gradually help him contain and overcome his fear and anxiety when he has to speak or perform in public. Or it may produce a paradoxical effect, whereby the patient fails to feel miserable during the assigned time. In fact, usually, as in the case of this manager, the harder one tries to feel bad, the less frightened one will become. This is the most frequent effect, and, in a similar fashion, we proceed to guide our patients to use this technique in order to cope with their most critical moments. We guide the patients to drive themselves to exasperation with their negative thoughts and feelings. The idea is to make them touch the bottom in order to come back to the surface every time they start to feel that they are "drowning" in their fear.

Furthermore, in this case we included an illusion of alternatives. In our second prescription, meant for the day of the presentation, we gave the patient the possibility of choice between two tasks: the first choice was very threatening and difficult to put in practice—declaring one's most tormenting secret; in comparison, the second seemed less frightening and easier to do—speak in public. Thus, we forced the person to commit to a task that, if presented as the only option, would have been probably considered insurmountable.

Even in those very rare cases when patients opt to declare their secret, the same result is obtained. Patients report that, soon after the "confession," all the tension evaporates, enabling them to carry out their speech or performance with remarkable tranquility. Unfortunately, the usual attempt to control one's tension leads to a loss of control.

On the contrary, when we declare our fragility, it becomes our point of strength. Our weakness can thus become a point of strength if it is not denied, but directed and used. The denial of our own fragility, expressed as a refusal to accept our own limitations and renunciations, makes our weakness unmanageable, and causes it to overwhelm us in certain situations. If, on the contrary, we not only accept our own fragility, but also prescribe it to ourselves, the effect will, most often, be a reduction in or even a cancellation of the negative results that the weakness might have produced.

We use the very process, which has led to the construction of a pathology but if re-oriented in the opposite direction, it would lead to its self-destruction: *"Similia similibus curantur."*

The secret lies in transforming something that we are subjected to into something that we manage. A person who calmly declares his fragility to others not only does not seem fragile, but comes across as strong, because we need much greater courage to declare than to hide our fragility.

Child behavior problems

A scholar from our institute (Fiorenza and Nardone 1995; Fiorenza 2000) has carried out a specific research on the resolution of child behavioral problems. During a period of three years, he has experimented on techniques for the most frequent child pathologies: hyperactivity, elective mutism, opposing, provocative, and aggressive behavior, and others.

Our intervention in this area of problems is based on a fundamental assumption: we avoid treating children directly. We have realized that in most cases direct treatment with children with behavioral problems became an attempted solution that made things worse rather than helped to solve the problems.

From our point of view, this reality is due to the self-fulfilling-prophecy process that is triggered when a child is brought and kept in therapy. In other words, when we make children come to therapy, we will be communicating to them that there is something wrong with them. This is the starting point of a pathological prophecy which the children and parents usually begin to believe in. If the parents and the child start believing that there is something pathological in the child's behavior, they will begin to behave accordingly, as if this were real, and probably end up fulfilling it.

Therefore, when dealing with child behavior problems, we choose to intervene in an indirect way by guiding the parents and sometimes even teachers to put into action certain maneuvers specifically devised to break the problematic behavioral patterns that maintain the situation.

Opposing and provocative behavior

A common child problem is the manifestation of opposing and provocative behavior, which can be limited to, for example, provocative use of vulgar expressions, compulsive repetition of good-luck phrases, or else, even more shocking, manifestations of aggressive violent attitudes, self-induced erotic pleasure, and self-harm. In such cases, we ask both parents and teachers to invite the child to exhibit his disturbing behavior several times a day as some kind of request to please the people around him.

The prescription is meant to have paradoxical effects, which, in the large majority of cases, do occur. By making the parents or teachers ask the child to exhibit a specific behavior we obtain a double effect. First, it helps to tranquilize the parents or teachers because they are now the ones requesting the behavior and thus feel in control of what was previously considered and explicitly treated as an inappropriate and disturbing behavior. Second, the child's disturbing behavior will be deprived of its spontaneity and its distressing properties, while placing the child in a double bind (Bateson et al., 1956; Watzlawick, Beavin, and Jackson, 1967; Sluzki and Ransom, 1976) with the illusion of a choice between (a) continuing with the behavior, which is now emptied of its significance since it is no longer involuntary and spontaneous, and (b) disobeying by going against the prescription and thus abandoning the disturbing behavior. Most often, the child will start refusing to act in this way, simply because he was told to do so.

Thus, already from the first therapeutic encounter with the parents or teachers, we will start seeing tangible results. So in line with the Chinese stratagem we encountered earlier, we put out the fire by adding wood. This paradoxical prescription brings us to reach the desired objective: that of reducing and eventually eliminating this disconcerting behavior.

Elective mutism

Indirect interventions are used also with children with elective mutism. This is a particular childhood problem whereby the child refuses to speak in certain social situations (for example, at home, at school, at play). Generally, the child suffering from this problem has normal linguistic abilities even though he/she tends to communicate by means of gestures, facial expressions, nodding, or short, monosyllable sounds.

Once more, therapy is carried out indirectly through the parents. In such cases, we invite the parents to reward their child on a daily basis with a token to thank him for not disturbing them, while avoiding giving him special attention throughout the rest of the time he stays silent. In this way, we give a positive connotation to the disorder, while removing the secondary advantages this disorder brought to the child.

Usually, such a maneuver is enough to change the undesirable behavior. In such cases the usual attempted solution is to give the child always more attention, since it is commonly believed that this mutism is given by lack of affection. Once more, this is a case that illustrates how the attempted solution tends to maintain and exacerbate the problem. By giving the child more attention, we are sustaining the problem, because the child gains secondary advantages from this behavior. Yet again, with all the good intentions, we produce the worse consequences.

Enuresis

Enuresis or bed wetting is another child problem that we efficaciously treat indirectly. Bed wetting is common among young children. However, it becomes a problem when this behavior persists beyond the (chronological and mental) age of five, when sphincter control has been reached. In our opinion, this behavior persists over time because it is maintained and sometimes nurtured by the very attempts to overcome it.

So, our first intervention is to identify the usual attempted solutions of the family members. In the majority of the cases, these oscillate between corrective and reassuring behavior. In other words, parents tend to get angry when they see that there has been another episode of bed wetting but then reassure the child and try to solve the problem by buying special gadgets, sleeping with the child to reassure him, washing the sheets in the middle of the night so that the child always has clean linen, and so forth. The child is corrected but is still kept from taking responsibility for his behavior.

We prescribe to the parents a true ordeal both for them and for their child. The parents are told to take it in turns to wake up the child every hour of the night, to monitor when the wetting takes place. Furthermore, it is specified that, when the bed is found wet, they have to get the child out of bed and together they change the sheets and hand-wash them carefully and then hang them to dry. Only then can they tuck in the child and let him go to sleep. This has to be carried out every time the bed is wet—even if this happens a hundred times.

The situation resolves itself immediately. Already in the next session a large percentage of parents report that bed wetting has been reduced to one or two episodes a week. The same regime is stuck to but the nocturnal wake-ups are reduced to every other hour, then to every three hours and so forth.

In all cases, our final intervention is to advise the parents to avoid the previous unsuccessful attempted solutions. Our ultimate aim is to turn the parents into the real therapists or problem solvers for their children. In most cases, we never actually meet the child.

Eliminating pathological labeling

Another frequent problem faced when working with child problems is pathological labeling. Unfortunately, it is very frequent that specialists in the field come to label erroneously a problematic behavior, and, in our opinion, they launch a prophecy that then fulfills itself. As Hobbes writes in *Behemoth*, "Prophecy is many times the principal cause of the events foretold."

An interesting case of wrong pathological labeling is that of seven-year-old Thomas. Thomas had been diagnosed with psychotic and autistic traits. His parents came to our clinic declaring that this was their last resort. They had been to various specialists, who all confirmed the initial diagnosis carried out by the child psychiatrist, who had carried out various tests on Thomas, who had begun to exhibit unintelligible communication, consisting of singsongs and repetition of verbal formulae and of behavioral rituals. He also talked out loud when on his own, while he avoided all sorts of social interaction.

It is important to note that the psychiatrist who first worked on this case, carried out a series of tests so that she could have some form of attestation to back up her request to have a facilitator to follow Thomas in class, to help him with his academic and relational difficulties. However, the parents report that, after the diagnosis and the various specialized interventions, Thomas's behavior got even worse.

Obviously, after such a diagnosis, which was confirmed over and over again by the various specialists, Thomas's parents felt helpless. Their attempts to control their child's bizarre behavior were limited to handing over and delegating the management of their child's problematic situation to teachers and other numerous specialists and caregivers. His father was something of an absent figure, since he worked in another town, while Thomas's mother had helplessly accepted the situation, and she limited herself to following the guidelines indicated to her by the school. She was advised to try out various punitive and corrective interventions to try to stop her son's bizarre behavior.

Everyone around Thomas knew of the situation and everyone tried to "help." Every one was checking on Thomas, treating him as the "poor incurable child". There was a whole network of caregivers that acted in this case: parents, close relatives and friends, school staff (class teacher, headmistress, Thomas's personal facilitator, etc.), the town's Health System Unit and all those who had come in contact with Thomas since his parents felt the need to seek help for his condition. All this "helped" to bring about an uncontrollable "Pygmalion effect"[18] in all spheres of Thomas's life: at home, at school, with specialists, and so forth. Once the expectation or the prophecy has been launched, it works as a confirmatory process that leads to its self-fulfillment.

As we explained earlier, we try to avoid making children come to therapy—especially in this case, where we could have been seen as just another agent, confirming the initial diagnosis (i.e. that the child was mentally ill). So we intervened indirectly, working exclusively with the parents.

The principal intervention was the reframing of the diagnosis. We understood that, as long as the agents around Thomas continued to believe he was a poor, incurable, autistic child, and treated him accordingly, and as long as they believed there was "no way out"

---

[18] Pygmalion effect, a term derived from the extensive research of Robert Rosenthal on the manner in which one's beliefs, biases, and expectations can have an impact on the phenomena under investigation. He used the expression "Pygmalion effect" to show the effects triggered by a given expectation. Rosenthal created intelligent scholars out of nothing by filling the teachers with the prophecy that they were particularly promising students, whereas actually they had been randomly selected. In the same way he was able to create good swimmers and rodents with very good explorative skills. In all these cases, he demonstrated the effects on behavior of having positive expectancies. However, not only he who retains positive expectancies but also he who retains negative expectancies can produce consequent effects out of nothing.

for Thomas, no changes could take place. Everyone treated him as an autistic child. They excused him and protected him—with the expectation of his sister. This is what we call a positive exception. She treated him as a brother, with whom she played and related at an equal level. She did not pity him or excuse his bizarre behavior.

Therapist: You have other children, true?

Father: Thomas has a sister.

Therapist: OK, and when he plays with his sister what does he do? He plays always in this way, fantasizing, or he plays in a more concrete way?

Mother: Er, he doesn't interact so much at school … and lately with his sister he fights a lot … but they play, they hug one another, they run after one another … they play hide and seek …

Therapist: However, while they play, they fight a lot. What do they fight about?

Mother: They fight. My daughter [with a reproaching tone] is very much nit-picking and is very vigilant of her belongings …

Father: Of her toys, games …

Mother: She always fights with him and sends him away. She tells him off, because she sees Thomas as someone who ruins her things, so sends him away. [She smiles.]

Father: Therefore, they don't play as brothers and sisters play: they are on two different wavelengths.

Therapist: OK, but if I understood right, otherwise please do correct me, Thomas's sister is the only person who treats him as if he was a normal child?

Mother: Yes, I try to treat him as if he was normal—that is, I try … I see that Thomas … maybe I blame myself a lot. I think that … Thomas has potentialities, even to learn … he rides the bike, he rollerblades ... he is intelligent in many things ... I observe that he has the potential to do all the normal things kids do ... even to read and write ... Even at school he does all the schoolwork. Obviously certain things he leaves out, but the things he wants to do he does them well. However, one day he writes and does things fine, another day he doesn't ... you can't program things with him. You can say OK we'll do this tomorrow, because one has to see whether he is willing to do stuff [smiling], and he is almost never so willing.

Therapist: However, you are telling me that beyond his words and numerical rituals he is competent just like other kids: to rid a bike, to rollerblade, intelligent, he understands things ...

Father: [Breaking in.] Yes, yes, he runs fast, he is smart, he kicks ...

Therapist: If he needs something for himself, he manages to do it tranquilly, no?

Father: Sometimes ...

Therapist: If he has to solve a problem for himself, for example he needs to buy something for himself, is he able to do so or not?

Mother: No, I don't trust Thomas alone. The first one not to let him is ... myself.

Therapist: I know that you don't trust him; but I asked whether he has confidence in himself! [Pause.] At least a bit!?

Mother: Thomas's needs are difficult to interpret., He might have the need to eat a hundred sweets and I tell him to eat just two a day ...

Father: But when he wants them, even when we place them somewhere high, he takes a chair or a ladder and he reaches out for them.

Mother: Oh, yes.

Therapist: OK, therefore he manages to solve problems.

Father: [nodding] When he wants, he works them out.

Mother: Yes, yes, I had hidden a box of chocolate, thinking that in this way he would not think about them much. Instead, he managed to find it, he manages to find everything, obviously those things that interest him [smiling] …

Therapist: Or, better still, he enjoys it even more [with a serious expression].

Father: Maybe [nodding].

Mother: No, he enjoys it more when you hide them from him.

Therapist: The more difficult they are, the more he enjoys it, right?

Father: Yes, yes [smiling].

Mother: He is truly … even a bit … he enervates you, he wears you out even because he has a very transparent expression … he has a splendid character …

Father: He is very radiant … immediately, one can understand whether he is happy or not …

So, our first intervention focused on reframing the parents' negative perception of Thomas. We launched another, more functional, prophecy.[19] From the questions asked, Thomas seemed like a seven-year-old child with difficulties but also with certain potentialities if he is given the opportunity. Once more, we did not try to directly convince and persuade Thomas's parents, but we limited ourselves to ask intervening, discriminating questions that made them arrive at this perception on their own. As indicated earlier, one of our most favorite philosophers, Blaise (1995), in his *Pensées* denotes, "People are generally better persuaded by the

---

[19] "Self-fulfilling prophecy" is a term used to refer to the fact that frequently things turn out just as one expected or prophesied that they would, not necessarily because of one's prescience but because one behaved in a manner that optimized these very outcomes. A teacher who predicts that a student will ultimately fail tends to treat that student in ways that increase the likelihood of failure, thus fulfilling the original prophecy.

reasons which they have themselves discovered than by those which have come into the mind of others."

At this point, it was important to identify the attempted solutions used by the parents and by others, which unfortunately, in spite of all the good intentions, maintain and worsen the situation.

Therapist: In all those diagnostic and therapeutic misadventures, were you ever given clear indications to follow on how to proceed with Thomas?

Father: Love him, stand by him, have patience …

Mother: Yes, not beat him, not yell at him …

Therapist: Fantastic [with a paradoxical tone].

Father: Yes … these.

Mother: But which, frankly [looking at her husband], you don't manage to do. You yell at him. We do not spank him … we never did that … maybe we threatened to do so in certain situations when he made us lose our temper but never came to do so …

Therapist: But regarding his rituals, what do you do? You let him be or you try to make him stop?

Father: [He nods at the latter option.] At least we try to tell him so.

Mother: I tell him to stop, that's enough, it's just that now he ends his rites with "that's enough."

Therapist: And he picked up "that's enough!"

Mother: And he continues saying the phrase …

Father: Or with numbers. I tell him I'm not interested and then he tells me they are seven but you are not interested.

Mother: And so he repeats it. Our interventions are useless …

Therapist: In fact, I think that you play his game! Just like when you hid the chocolates …

Mother: Now I try not to reply back. I do not answer him back … So he tests me to see whether I really stop responding … at first I did not reply … they are things that work for a while but then he finds a way out …

Therapist: What do you expect from us?

Father: Help … lately I haven't seen any progress.

Therapist: In what you have been told to do?

Mother: I have tried to put trust in the *dottoressa* [female doctor] who follows Thomas …

Father: We are still hoping.

Mother: We have left everything to them … we do not know exactly what they are doing, he used to do horse riding, we have tried that … Then they stopped it. The reason was, they said, that Thomas did not want to stay with animals, he is not interested in animals …

Father: he was more interested in playing with Peter the instructor.

Therapist: OK, therefore [pause], I would like to propose to you some sort of game. Your son is proposing to you certain games; I'm proposing to you another, OK? It seems to me that the game that the entire world around Thomas is playing, sets off from the presumption that Thomas has a mental disorder so severe that is so difficult to treat. That is called autism, right? Therefore, specific therapy for autism was used but had no effect on Thomas, right?

Mother: No, nothing worked.

Therapist: OK.

Father: Or let's say very scarce results.

Therapist: OK, so have you every doubted that this game is not the right game for Thomas?

Mother: Oh, yes.

Father: We're here because of that.

Therapist: And the game might commence by thinking that Thomas is not autistic? [Pause.] And that we should start doing something for a child who is affected by an incurable mental illness but of a disorder that is treatable?

Father: [with a pleading tone] This is our dream.

Mother: Because he [referring to the husband] has even looked it up on the Internet. He managed to find—[The husband dismissed her words with a gesture, as if to say this was irrelevant.]

Therapist: However, all this has to go through you! We need your help!

Father: Well … if we're here …

When working with children, it is of paramount importance to turn the parents into co-therapist. Parents should not be dismissed or blamed. We have to make them aware that it is only through their help that we can activate change in their children. Nobody can substitute for them.

Therapist: We want to try to help but we have to give ourselves a limited time. You see, not years but ten sessions [pause], not a session more if we do not see results because this will mean that our attempt, the method, does not work. We don't want to become accomplices of a pathology by continuing to see a family, a child, for years, or even more—we render it more pathogenic. If within ten sessions we do not see results, we will interrupt the therapy. If we see results, we obviously proceed. Normally, within this period of time, we see results. However, I do not know whether this will be your case. However, my personal style and that of my collaborators … we do not make children undergo therapy. But we see the parents of the children. Not because they need a cure themselves but to guide them to cure their children. [Both parents nod and smile.] In the sense that when one assumes that a child has a pathology, and he is treated as pathological, normally if he isn't, he is made so. Everyone behaves as if Thomas was so, therefore we end up rendering him like that. [Parents nod.]

Mother: Can I speak?

Therapist: Feel free.

Mother: In fact this is the point, is it true? [She looks at her husband.] He seems more autistic now [smiling] than when he started saying … than before, before he did not … [smiling]

Therapist: It's obvious, if a child is treating as Thomas is, as autistic, and everyone believes that he is so, everyone will start looking at him as if he was truly autistic, and finally the prophecy comes true. Therefore, we need to start playing a completely different game.[20] [Pause.]

Father: Excuse me, we are the players in this game?

Therapist: Yes. Therefore, it is about making you do things with him, but you have to do them, nobody can take your place. [Pause.] For more than ten years we have avoided seeing children directly in therapy. We give indications to parents, we guide the parents. First, because, in our opinion, if we make a child undergo therapy we are already "pathologizing" him, we are already creating "the case." Kids take up this prophecy and fulfill it. Furthermore, parents need to be taught how to behave with their children—we cannot substitute for them. This is our hypothesis. This is to tell you that the game I would like to propose to you, it is a game where we hypothesize, as a game, that your child is not autistic, but has a serious of disorders that can be changed through the practice of strategies, but through

---

[20] The therapist's choice of the word "game" instead of pathology, mental disorder, diagnosis, etc., is intentional, to start depathologising Thomas's situation.

you ... However this will require a lot of effort from you. [Pause.]

Mother: Now he is away [referring to the father], he won't be around so much; practically, there is only me.

Therapist: Perfect. Well, well ...

Father: However, I'm home every fourth night.

Therapist: Well, but they have to take place on a daily basis [addressing the mother] and then even when there is you [to the father] it is better because you reinforce it even more. Then, when you move to R—, there will be both of you, right?

Father: Yes.

Therapist: Well, perfect, OK? [Looks first at the father then at the mother.] Therefore, the first idea is this: if your son did not have an autistic disorder, represented by an enclosure in his own world, which is not the case [short pause], but he had a serious of disorders based on fixations, on rituals, OK? The best way to intervene would be further ritualizing his ritual.

Father: That is ...?

Therapist: OK, in practical terms [addressing the mother], how much of the day is your son with you?

Mother: Ah, my son is at home from lunchtime, that is around noon ... until bed time, nine thirty, ten or even eleven.

Therapist: Well, OK, perfect. At every strike of the hour, from now till the next session in two weeks' time, at one, then at two, three ... at every hour of the day [pause], you have to call your son, and ask him to carry out for five minutes one of his singsongs, or his numerical formulae, et cetera, and you have to stay there to observe him just like a spectator. Better still, call your daughter if she is home; and tell him, "Now we'll watch you do it." [Pause.] Every hour, for five minutes you ask him to give his performance. Once the five minutes are through,

135

throughout the successive fifty-five minutes, you have to avoid any sort of intervention [pause] on Thomas's problems; or, rather you have to avoid all sort of corrective intervention ... to his rituals ... [Pause.]

Father: Even if he is doing actions that are undoubtedly wrong?

Therapist: Yes. You have every hour for five minutes together with your daughter, otherwise alone. Ask him to step up on his stage and carry out his show. During the successive fifty-five minutes, avoid hanging around, ready to intervene when he does wrong, but hand him back the responsibility for his actions.

Mother: Yes, I belief this is better if I carry this out once home, make him stay indoors ...

Father: [to the mother] Every hour, this means whether you're indoors or not, always ...

Therapist: However if you don't ask him yourself, he will do it on his own, right?

Mother: Yes, yes [smiling].

Therapist: At least you will be asking.

Mother: Yes, true. But if we're out and about then he goes in the middle of the road or he does something ...

Therapist: Obviously, I'm not asking you to—

Father: [addressing the mother] Of course, if he got run over by a car ...

Therapist: Obviously, the safety of your son and daughter, that is evident! But otherwise you have to frustrate [pause] his symptoms. Or, better so, avoid showing him that you continuously bite at his hook. Let's presume that your son is a small rascal that holds you hostage [pause], OK?

Mother: Yes.

Therapist: Therefore how should one react? One should try not to be tricked every time by his rituals. You would hand it back to him [pause], agree?

Father: We start off today?

Therapist: Yes, from today. Therefore there will be days where [to the father] you will be present. In these occasions when you will be all present, call him: "Please, Thomas, let us watch you ..." OK? [Both parents nod.] Every hour for five minutes. Outside this time, you have to avoid all sort of corrective intervention or to speak to him about his problem, as if [pause] the problem was no longer present. We would like to see what happens next, during the two weeks, OK?

We started seeding doubt of whether Thomas's behaviors were actually manifestations of psychotic and autistic traits or whether this was a prophecy that was fulfilling itself. Through the use of the strategic dialogue, we launched another prophecy by pointing out that Thomas's behavior seemed more similar to the ritualistic actions carried out by individuals who suffer of obsessive-compulsive disorder: the singsongs, repetitions of verbal formulas, and particular actions. This was a turning point because, unlike psychotic traits, obsessive-compulsive behavior is treatable. The perception changed. Before coming to therapy, Thomas's parents perceived their son's situation as a hopeless case of an incurable psychotic illness, and this made them feel helpless.

Through the use of intervening and discriminating questions and paraphrasing, we made the parents come to perceive Thomas no longer as a fragile untreatable child, but as a small, smart rascal who gains secondary advantages out of his "problematic" situation, who exploits his parents' sense of helplessness to avoid doing stuff he detests, while using his exasperating compulsive behavior to blackmail them and acquire all that he desires.

Thus, following this premise, we introduced a prescription based on the logic of paradox: we invited the mother to ask her son to exhibit his "comedy" every hour. In other words, we used a paradoxical injunction to request the behavior that we wished to stop. This deprives the undesired behavior of its spontaneity and places

Thomas in a double-bind position (Bateson et al, 1956; Watzlawick, Beavin, and Jackson, 1967; Sluzki and Ransom, 1976). If he complies with his mother's request, that is, he continues with his behavior, his "comedy" will no longer be the same as before because his behavior will be emptied of its significance, since it is no longer involuntary and spontaneous but intended and requested by the mother. So, in such case, he will be acting according to his mother's control and no longer his, and this normally leads to a gradual cessation of the behavior. On the other hand, if he disobeys and rebels against the prescription, he will end up abandoning the undesirable behavior and we will reach immediately and precisely our objective. In other words, in both cases the undesirable behavior leads to its cancellation.

Furthermore, we introduced the conspiracy of silence regarding Thomas's problem throughout the rest of the day.

The effects of our first intervention were immediately visible. Already after the first session, Thomas had recovered an intelligible communication. His parents reported that after a couple of days, when they asked for the exhibit and observed without intervening throughout the rest of the day, Thomas stopped his singsongs and numerical formulas to take up a more comprehensible language. His mother admitted that Thomas was much more caring and calmer with her.

In the second session, we noticed a significant change in Thomas's mother, who seemed much more confident in her abilities in managing her son's symptomatology. The paradoxical prescription led Thomas to stop his undesirable behavior but it also helped the mother feel more in control of the situation. During our second encounter, we observed a positive reorientation of the expectations in both parents. This led to improvements, which were noticed also by the teachers at school. We were astonished by the drastic change in the parents' attitude toward their son. They now treated him as an intelligent child with compulsive problems and no longer as the mentally ill child in need of protection. Moreover, the mother was confident that they should halt Thomas's individual psychotherapy with the child psychiatrist. She said that Thomas had been quite obedient and calm throughout the entire two weeks but showed signs of uneasiness after their last appointment with the psychiatrist. We agreed with such a request, since the child had been undergoing individual psychotherapy for more than a year without any positive outcomes.

During the third phase, our efforts were focused on consolidating the obtained results; in reinforcing the realization of the new prophecy. The same prescriptions were kept: conspiracy of silence and the "comedy" exhibition. The latter was first reduced to every two hours, then every three hours, then every four and so forth. However, even though Thomas had at this point reduced his compulsive behavior close to zero, it was necessary to continue and consolidate the obtained results. Furthermore, the parents were invited to use the same paradoxical technique when Thomas took up his provocative behavior spontaneously: they had to ask him to do it and do it better. However, this happened in infrequent situations where Thomas believed that his parents would still fall victims of his treats, e.g. in front of friends, at mass and other situations where Thomas's behavior would have been of embarrassment to the parents. The parents were told to note down these episodes in a "ritual diary." The ritual diary has the same objective as the log prescription given to the obsessive-phobic patients. The parents were encouraged to think that this task was meant to monitor the infrequent yet critical situations, while in reality the use of this diary was meant to limit the parents' intervention in correcting Thomas's behavior, by making them shift their attention onto the task given.

In order to increment Thomas's responsible behavior and autonomy, we invited the parents to ask Thomas for small favors every day, something small but something new. This prescription is based on the as-if technique: that is the parents were invited to ask a favor from Thomas *as if* they were sure their son was capable of doing it. To the parents' surprise Thomas was eager to carry out these small tasks: giving a "small" hand at home, helping his father cook, helping his mum while doing shopping, etc.

The only thing that still preoccupied these parents was Thomas's solitary "monologues." They said that often they observed Thomas in his room speaking to himself. On close examination of the situation, it appeared that Thomas had created an imaginary friend with whom he would play, read, talk, etc. We invited the parents to observe more closely these events and to take part in this "imaginary game." We explained that playing with imaginary friends is a very usual and normal game at this age, and that this behavior should not be confused with depersonalization symptomatology, as they had been encouraged to think by the other helping agents.

During the following session, the parents reported that Thomas was very reluctant to let them join in his imaginary games. They reported that at first Peter—the imaginary character invented by their son—was very much present in their games but after some days Thomas had played with them and his sister without any reference to Peter.

Even the teachers at school noticed a major change in Thomas's behavior and requested that the parents ask us for tips for them to follow. We invited the parents to tell the teachers that we held a different opinion regarding Thomas's behavior and that this hypothesis was being confirmed by the results obtained. We encouraged them to inform them about the immediate results they obtained by the application of the paradoxical prescription, so that the teachers could make use of it even at school.

The teachers followed the indications and in a couple of days they observed the same phenomenon even at school. Thomas stopped exhibiting his compulsive behavior, exhibited intelligible communication, and started to interact and play with children of his age. Furthermore, his parents allowed him to take up a sport, swimming, which helped him to make more friends and gain more self-confidence.

Even the caregivers at the Health System Unit noticed the "magical" change, and they also started doubting whether the diagnosis made two years earlier was still valid. After a couple of months the diagnosis was changed and the Health System Unit also attested that Thomas's progress was so significant that he no longer required the assistance of a facilitator.

So, to sum up, the core of this therapy was that of changing the diagnosis, of changing the prophecy. Thus, in order to remove the pathological labeling, we had to create a different context around

Thomas, by presenting to the parents, teachers, caregivers, etc. a new perception of this seven-year-old. We had launched another prophecy, which slowly, slowly led to its own fulfillment.

Compared with other children of his age group, Thomas still shows deficits in knowledge, but this is a pedagogical and not a psychopathological problem.

Changing prophecies, from dysfunctional to functional, is an intervention, we employ not only with children but also with adults, as we proceed to show in the next section.

Presumed psychosis

We use the term *presumed psychosis* because we believe that often a wrong diagnosis of psychosis is conducted, and that it is this labeling that eventually "invents" the illness (Nardone and Portelli, 2005). From our point of view, to assume from the very beginning that a patient is psychotic means, to be caught up in a prophecy that sees no or very little possibility in treating the patient. We strongly believe that a therapist should always try to do something to alleviate the suffering of the patient and his/her loved ones, even when the case is considered clinically untreatable.

By saying it is a psychotic case, the therapist, like all the other agents around the patient, can be easily caught up by a consequential overwhelming feeling of helplessness. As Watzlawick used to say "words are like bullets"—and they are, without doubt, responsible for the construction of one's reality.

The word "presumed" sheds a ray of hope and thus one feels that something might still be done. Then, if the treatment works well and the patient recovers from his psychotic symptoms, we can affirm that it was no case of psychosis, if not, at least we have tried our best to better the situation and often small positive changes still take place that help the patient and his beloved ones adjust better. But, again, we come to discover a problem by means of its solution: "Knowing through changing."

At our Center we have had many diagnosed psychotic patients who have completely overcome their presumed psychosis. In saying this, we do not mean that we have healed psychotic patients, but only shown through successful therapies that these persons were not afflicted by a real psychosis but by invalidating symptoms defined as signs of psychosis in traditional nosographic classifications.

Having clarified this fundamental assumption, we can now proceed in presenting the phases of therapy in the treatment of these highly intimidating patients.

In the first stage of treatment, the most important therapeutic action is the complete acceptance of the distorted reality presented by the patient, as if it were actually real. In order to do this, the therapist needs to trace the logic of the patient and use his language. At a communicative, relational, and strategic level, the therapist needs to follow the patient's narration of his reality, without alienating himself to what the patient is saying, and thus openly show that he acknowledges his suffering. This permits the therapist to establish a good and suggestive relationship with the patient and also with his family.

Once this is accomplished the first session goes into the second stage of therapy: to construct and introduce an invented reality, which realizes concrete results. In other words, the therapist must build a therapeutic representation usually followed by a ritual prescription that fits with the pathological patient's perception and reaction, which drives it toward self-destruction.

This amounts to a strategic form of art on the therapist's part, because he first has to follow the logic and structure of the patient's representation of reality, then invent and introduce something tailored to patient's non-ordinary logic, capable of achieving an effective change. This normally takes up the entire first session, so as to be able to make this new representation, based on the patient's logic, more credible, more artistic and "real" for the patient. The representations of reality, or the delusions, of patients with presumed psychosis follow a non-ordinary logic. To be able to alter their dysfunctional balance, we cannot disregard the patient's delusions but, in devising therapeutic strategies, we need to use the non-ordinary logic that underlies these specific delusions. In other words, the therapist needs to follow the seemingly crazy logic that underlies the patient's ideas and actions by inexplicitly showing the patient that what he is thinking and doing makes sense, while gently intervening by sowing seeds of doubt in what the patient has always held as absolute. This should be done with great caution so as not to dispel his delusions.[21] On the contrary, the therapist should make use of counter-delusions to introduce some different aspects that serve to divert the delusion toward a new, more functional balance but without driving out the old convictions.

Furthermore, we need to modify the dynamics within the patient's interactive system with others and the world. This is carried out by the prescriptions such as the Conspiracy of Silence, the Nightly Family Ritual (both prescriptions have been already described in previous sections) and others, which help frustrate the secondary advantages offered by the symptoms.

The third and fourth stages of therapy are the same as previously described treatment protocols: guiding the person and the family to build a new balance based on the new reality after an often dramatic change. For the sake of clarification, we will use real clinical examples.

Riccardo, a shabbily dressed, bearded twenty-year-old, was brought to therapy by his father for his bizarre attitude, which had been diagnosed as "monomaniac behavior." Two years earlier he started attending university, where he joined the Socialist Revolutionary Political party, which became his sole and exclusive interest and encapsulated his entire existence. He left home, because he was truly convinced that the family was a social constriction that suffocated personal growth and self-fulfillment, to join party comrades at the university campus, but failed to attend lectures. His entire existence whirled around political issues and debates. He would isolate himself for days to study political treatises and texts.

---

[21] The classical definition of delusion is a false, personal belief, based on incorrect inferences regarding external reality, which is firmly upheld by the individual despite everyone else's contrary believes.

His conversations with family members and flatmates were monothematic. He would passionately lecture and try to convince others of his political ideologies, while losing his temper when others objected. He was hospitalized a number of times because he had undergone critical moments when his behavior had gone out of control. His father tried to talk sense into him while his party comrades avoided him, annoyed by his bizarre behavior and repetitive speeches. He came to therapy depressed but not defeated by his failed attempts to be taken back by the party.

This was a fundamental aspect that we recognized as useful so as to be able to divert the patient's delusion to a more functional balance. This was the right lever to exploit, since he wanted, more than anything else in the world, to be taken back by the group. But the patient was convinced that to be reaccepted by the group he had to find more persuasive words. Thus, his attempted solutions were to study more about his ideology and then preach his knowledge to show his full commitment to the revolution and to the party. This was his conviction, his delusion. During the first session, it became clear that the patient would have done anything to be taken back by his party. We showed him that we could help him. And yet, following the logic of his delusion, we started sowing doubts about whether finding more persuasive words was actually the right way to be accepted back into the group.

Therapist: So the group does not want you anymore?

Patient: No, no.

Therapist: OK. But what are you doing so that you can get back to your group, so that you are accepted once more?

Patient: Yeah, in fact, that is what I need to understand … I need to understand better what I need to do.

Therapist: Hmm, but what have you done till now so that they would take you back?

Patient: No, I mean, that is no … continuing in this way, for example, I don't know, doing my best to diffuse the left-wing ideology …

in all schools, however, within normal limits, like others do, within normality …

Therapist: Hmm [nodding], and this is all that interests you? There is nothing else in your life?

Patient: Right now, no.

Therapist: So, when you can't meet people, you have your texts, which you study in great depth so that you will be well up in them? Do you speak about your texts with anyone or you keep them to yourself?

Patient: Yes, I do, but then people speak less to me, they become rubber walls (an Italian expression meaning words just bounce back off people; people do not understand) … I come to face rubber walls.

Therapist: So, you try to speak to them but they refuse you, therefore the more you speak the more they refuse you.

Patient: It's a great mess.

Therapist: So, correct me if I'm wrong but trying to convince them with words is the best way to draw them always more away from you?!

Patient: Yes, in fact …

Therapist: However, for you, the desire to profess your faith, your ideology … is uncontrollable … or else you have come to understand that the more you speak the more this distances you from them … What do you think is best now?

Patient: Now it's best to calm down a bit.

Therapist: Are you able to do so?

Patient: Yes. However, I manage quite poorly.

Therapist: Well, I'll help, OK? [Pause.] Well, when they keep you away, this provokes in you depressive moments, i.e. you feel bad that they ignore you or you get angry?

Patient: I get angry and bury myself in my books.

Therapist: As if like saying, "Since you people are like that … I'll isolate myself and read, or else …"

Patient: Look for others.

Therapist: Others?

Patient: Yes, others, who knew what was happening in my life but who led their own tranquil life …

Therapist: But these people listen to you for five minutes and then they send you away and tell you to go to hell.

Patient: Yes, they greet me, "Hi, Riccardo"—and that's it.

Therapist: Or maybe even if they see you around, they would try to avoid you.

Father: He's monothematic.

Therapist: Monothematic. However, you have come to comprehend that the more you run after them, the more they run away.

Patient: The more they run away …

Therapist: You said that you would like to speak up, state your case, but nobody is now willing to listen to you …

Patient: Yes.

Therapist: Or else they listen to you for five minutes and then they tell you to go to hell? On the other hand when you talk to your dad, your dad discusses it with you? But after a while you will start to quarrel, true?

Father: We do not quarrel: we discuss.

Therapist: You start to quarrel because you [toward the father] are not so much in agreement with his ideas. You get into a sort of political debate ... and you clash ...

Father: [Nods.]

Therapist: OK, we would like you to follow our indications to the letter, that is, we would like you to allow a precise period of time for your orations. We would like you to give out a speech every day while [speaking to the father] you and your wife are his presence. Therefore, what we would like you to do during the coming two weeks, every evening, you get together in your living room, you and your wife seated in absolute silence, you [pointing to the patient] standing. You set an alarm clock to ring after half an hour, because your speech should be managed within an adequate period of time and you, for half an hour, should carry out your speech on a chosen argument regarding your ideology and for half an hour you have to stand there and give out your speech—talk and talk. You and your wife [referring to the father] should remain the entire half an hour in absolute silence. When the alarm rings, stop, it's all over ... until the following evening you have to avoid to speech about your ideology and studies ... you have to keep what we call conspiracy of silence: you [to the father] have to really avoid it if it happens that he starts speaking. Tell him, "Tell us about it this evening during the half an hour." Postpone it. Riccardo, this goes for everyone. I mean, during the coming two weeks we would like you to restrict your need to speak about this important thing to the half-hour. Therefore, we would like you to avoid speaking about it with anyone—after all nobody really listens to you, they avoid you! But since you feel the need to express your faith, your belief ... you will do so with them [pointing at the parents]; for now let us limit ourselves to at least educate them. Let us start off from this first stage so that we can then move onto the rest, you agree?

Patient: Yes, yes.

147

The following session, Riccardo reported that he followed the prescription and that every evening, in just half an hour, he managed to develop his speech and bring it to a closure. He also declared that, besides the half-hour oration, he did not try to persuade the world of the revolution. He said he kept at heart what we had said the previous session. So, on meeting his friends, especially a female friend, he avoided speaking about his revolutionary ideology and he noticed that people started to hang around with him more.

The prescription also changed the family dynamic. Both Riccardo and his dad said that they had more tranquil days, when they spoke about sport, cinema, university, and other topics that had hitherto always been put aside to leave space for their usual political debates. At the end of the second session Riccardo was invited to continue giving out his speeches during the half-hour once a day, underlying their fundamental didactic purpose, while keeping a silence throughout the rest of the day just as he had managed to do so far. Furthermore, he was asked to carry out an experiment. We told him, "At a specific hour of the day, which you are free to choose, we want you to ask yourself, 'What would I do with my time if I were no longer interested in my revolution project? How would I spend my time differently from what I do now, if I were no longer interested in the revolution?' And for an hour every day, not more than an hour, carry it out. Let's see what you would choose to do for an hour a day, just an hour, not more, as if you were no longer interested in the revolution."

The patient arrived at the third session gladly itemizing all the new things he managed to do during the past two weeks. He confessed that he even had a date with a girl he liked, when they spent a pleasant evening talking about sweet nothings. Furthermore, during the last week, he felt the need to start reading other books such as novels.

Even though the as-if prescription was limited to just an hour a day, it triggered off what Thom (1990) has called the "butterfly effect" (which we touched on earlier) throughout the patient's entire daily routine. At the end of the session he claimed that, even though he was still loyal to his ideals, he thought that, every now and then, one had to take one's mind off things.

Patient: Well, observing other people's daily activities, even though they have not taken big life decisions—however, they have chosen their life—each one of them has an occupation or something else ... but they try to take their minds off it by doing something else. For me life was just commitment to my ideals and that's it. Then I tried to understand what other people do in their free time, go to the cinema, read novels and magazines ...

Therapist: Therefore, what you are saying is that what you previously considered as antirevolutionary miseries ... now you look at them differently?

Patient: That is, not as antirevolutionary but as a form of distracting, uninterested attitude ... now I'm trying to be more interested in art, there are so many beautiful things here in Tuscany, even in Arezzo, Piero della Francesca ...

Therapist: Not only, Poliziano and others.

Patient: I know. In fact this brings to mind ... even linking this to the commitment of certain historical leaders such as Trotsky and Lenin when they visited London. Lenin said, "Look, Westminster, it is wonderful." But Trotsky showed no interest: "No, I want to look at Russia ... just let me be." He did not want to see ...

Therapist: He did not want to see beyond his ideology. Therefore, you mean that your boundaries are getting elastic, more flexible?

Patient: Yes, a bit, yes.

During the following sessions, Riccardo reported that he went back to university, that he was dating other girls and that he no longer needed the half-hour podium. At home they finally had pleasant conversations. Every time, we acknowledged Riccardo's good work but suggested he continue with the prescriptions, each time increasing the length of the as-if session by an hour. This was fundamental at this stage, where we needed not to be blinded by results but work to consolidate the results achieved so far.

At the fifth session, we asked him to continue observing others just as anthropologists do, so that he would get to know more about others, especially about the female world, so that he would come to understand better what to do to enhance his practical capability. We also started working on his appearance, which still had something of the "revolutionary" about it, giving him some problems when he approached others. He was very rather taken by Oscar Wilde's maxim that it is only superficial people who don't judge by appearances. A "new" Riccardo arrived at the next session: he had shaved his beard, trimmed his hair and wore a clean T-shirt and a pair of denim jeans; he also looked and behaved his age, as a handsome, pleasant twenty-year-old.

Another exemplary case is of another twenty-year-old (whom we shall call Roberto) who arrived at our center with his parents after having been to various specialists in the field, who held divergent opinions and diagnoses of his "mental state." For more than five years, Roberto had segregated himself within a sector of his parents' mansion because he feared that certain people such as the handicapped, old people, and also his own brother would draw "beneficial energy" out of him. So, he avoided all sort of contact with the outside world and the few times he eventually went out he would perform some sort of "preventive ritual" before leaving the house and then a "repairing ritual" on his return to block the "draining process." But, since his brother still lived at home with them, for Roberto the danger was also inside the house, so the family—even though at first they tried to convince him of how much his brother loved him and that he should not be afraid of him—finally gave up and proceeded partitioned the house to prevent the two brothers from meeting.

However, the curious aspect of this case was that therapy began *before* our first encounter. Before coming to us, Roberto had read various books about our approach and treatment and so, in the time span between his call to fix the appointment and our actual meeting, he had tried to face his fear and embraced his brother, but this frightened him even more, so he had decided not to do it again.

Once more, our intervention was first to follow the patient's seemingly "crazy logic," enter his delusion by utilizing his same language, identify the attempted solutions put into operation by the patient and also by the family that maintained and worsened the situation, and then proceed to block the attempted solutions, by sowing a seed of doubt in the patient's convictions, and then proceed to find a creative yet credible way of turning the logic against itself.

Therapist: And yet you did something you were afraid to do before: you touched and embraced your brother and he did not drain all your beneficial energy? How do you explain this?

Patient: I don't know.

Therapist: Therefore, you have, till now, held a wrong idea. Until now, you have protected yourself from him. You could not even stand to see him, thinking that if you touched him he would suck out your beneficial energy. Now you have touched him and nothing happened ... on the contrary you we able to hold it back, true? Let me explain to you one thing. In such situations as this, when you feel that some sort of osmosis takes place, where beneficial energy passes from you to your brother— OK?—what one tends to rationally do is to think, "I need to defend myself by avoiding such situations; therefore, I need to avoid him; I should avoid to touch him, to even look at him." Or, better still, you have come to practice total avoidance.

Patient: What?

Therapist: You had come to a point where you had constructed extreme evasion ... you could not even stand to see him. Unfortunately, this rational reaction does not function. Because, in case of energy influx, the more you run away, the more energy gets lost ... so if you want to learn how to keep your beneficial energy, you need to gradually start doing the very opposite ... the more you avoid the feared situation—that is the more you avoid your brother, afraid that he would drain energy from you—the more energy will get lost by itself and passes on to him. In fact, when you embraced your brother, you did not lose all your beneficial energy, true?

Patient: No, I did not lose all my energy.

151

Therapist: OK.

Patient: But then I decided not to embrace him anymore because … when I was in the car getting here, I thought about my brother and energy escaped out of me …

Therapist: Be careful! It escaped without his being present. You have imagined it. Once more you did everything by yourself. Just think that during the past years, in reality, you've built your own trap, which you've got into but can't get out of. In what way? By avoiding confronting something that could have enabled you to hold in your beneficial energy. Instead, running away has made you weaker and weaker, so weak that energy gets lost by itself. Now to fortify yourself … we are very glad that we can start doing this with you from today because you have already set in motion a great change while you were waiting to come here. You have spontaneously found your way out. Now we have to proceed without getting frightened and return to the trap. In these days, you have to get used to gradually holding within you your beneficial energy, by gradually coming into contact with your brother. From now till the next time we meet, we would like you, every morning, to wake up and embrace your brother before he goes to work. OK? When he gets back, embrace him once more and then before going to bed. You have to keep in mind that this is the first step, which you discovered spontaneously, in starting to hold in your energy. By running way—

Patient: But I have to give him my energy?

Therapist: No, you will hold it within you. This will help you keep it for yourself and not give it to him. Before, by running away, by hiding, by avoiding contact, you were always making yourself weaker and weaker and energy passed to him. You are right in wanting to keep your energy and the attention of your parents to yourself. He has his own, he has other things … and the same goes for the outside world … do the same thing, OK? Besides this ritual, you [addressing the parents] should avoid—from now till the time we meet again—talking or asking about his fears. The more you speak about it, the more you work together to overcome it, the weaker Roberto becomes. So, throughout the day, you should keep what we call conspiracy of silence. You should avoid speaking about his fear and diffi- culties, or else this will exacerbate them, OK? You will get weaker and beneficial energy will get lost. But in the evenings, after dinner, get together all the family in the living room, get an alarm clock and set it to ring after half an hour, during which you [to the parents] will remain seated in absolute silence, and you, Roberto, standing. You will tell them all about the fears you felt throughout that day, all your worries, all those things that disturbed you. You [referring to the parents] should listen in absolute silence. When the alarm rings, stop—it is all over. Until the following evening avoid speaking about it.

Mother: There has to be his brother too?

Therapist: I would prefer the brother to be present too … so that in this way you fortify yourself even more … OK? And why not? In this way we send him some unbeneficial energy, the other type … no? [Everyone bursts into laughter.] But do not let him know, OK? We won't tell him.

Patient: OK, we won't tell him [laughing].

The family arrived the next session overwhelmed by the "miracu- lous" change that took place. They reported that Roberto carried out the (counter-) ritual three times a day throughout the entire two weeks, without fearing his brother; on the contrary, Roberto starting looking forward to his brother's return from work, when they spent time chatting, watching TV, playing with videogames, etc. Furthermore, from the following session, Roberto was seen alone in therapy, and reported that he had started going out, going to the gym (with his mum), and to mass, and was eager to go back to school the following academic year. On one of his outings, he had meet a disabled child whom he hugged lovingly, and, in ther- apy, he exclaimed that he could not understand why he used to fear handicapped people—they were so unfortunate and yet so caring. The rest of the therapy focused on establishing a new, more functional equilibrium both for Roberto and for the entire family. It is necessary to consolidate successes that have already been gained, so, by the end of the ten sessions, we had started working with the patient in developing social skills.

These clinical examples show that even such severe disorders can be treated in a short time, without recourse to traditional therapy. We do not "eliminate the delusion" but direct it toward its self-destruction. The principle that forms the basis of our treatment with presumed psychosis is "to add so as to reduce." Our intervention aims to circumvent the patient's resistance (Type 4 resistance—patient unable to collaborate) and to lead him to change his perception of reality. We use his own logic and mode of representing reality, and lead him through a series of "corrective" emotional experiences, until he begins to doubt his previously inflexible convictions.

As Goethe wrote, things are actually much simpler than one might think, but much more complicated than one might realize.

Chapter 7

Integrating Science into Practice

*"Unless you try to do something beyond what you have already mastered,
you will never grow".*
Ralph Waldo Emerson

Science and practice: research in clinical field

The purpose of this chapter is to recapitulate and provide a trenchant evaluation of the efforts put into the study of psychotherapy, while advancing possible alternatives for the study of effective and efficacious therapy. Naturally, no singular work presumes to address every contribution made in this field of study and this chapter is no exception. Finally, we will expose the intervention-research method used at the Centro di Terapia Strategica (CTS), which is in continuous evolution.

In the past decade, the integration of practice and science has become a major concern and the dominant commitment of most clinical scientists. This movement was triggered off by the always growing investment in managed care and in the health sector, which demanded greater accountability and improvements in clinical practice.

Since its foundation, the CTS has always endorsed the importance of giving equal weight to science and practice. Even though we always regarded research as an essential means of making our clinical work more effective, we never came to play part in that group of scientists who vowed to scientific faith, while forgetting that we are first and foremost, practitioners whose prime responsibility is to help those who ask our assistance.

155

Western, Novotny, and Thompson-Brenner (2004a) maintain that "the idea of creating a list of empirically supported psychosocial treatments was a compelling one, spurred in part by concerns about other widely disseminated practice guidelines that gave priority to pharmacotherapy over psychotherapy in the absence of evidence supporting such priority" (p. 632). This growing concern called for effective research that goes beyond describing what clinicians do in everyday practice, but that develops "measurable" means that can help obtain more useful treatments.

The first research approach that was promoted internationally in order to reduce the gap between research and practice was evidence-based clinical practice[22] (Chambless and Hollon, 1998), which followed the approach of evidence-based medicine. In the USA, a task force was formed, which came up with a list of "empirically supported treatments" (APA, 1995). This provoked disquiet among researchers and practitioners alike (Elliot, 1998). The controversy stemmed from the attempts of some clinical scientists to dictate which therapies could be retained as "acceptable" practice and which not.

Critics argued that the task force used very narrow definition of empirical research (Taylor, 1998; Henry, 1998). Qualitative research and case studies have long been a valuable part of the empirical foundation for psychotherapy but were demeaned or ignored by many for whom "empirical validation" equates to "randomised clinical trial RCT" (Koocher, 2003).

Starcevic (2003) was among those who perceive this method as very inappropriate in the study of the efficiency and efficacy of psychological treatments. Evidence-based mental health has treated psychological and pharmacological interventions identically in its search for best evidence of what works in the mental-health field (Parry, 2000).

---

[22] They are treatments that are tested with randomized controlled clinical trials (RCTs) (Herbert, 2003; Morrison, Bradley, and Western, 2003). "Randomized controlled trials" are a methodological procedure that compares groups of patients: experimental groups and placebo groups who receive no active treatment, in order to establish the usefulness of the treatment examined.

We agree with Goldfried and Eubanks-Carter (2004), who claim that the field's reliance on the medical model and manual-based interventions has contributed to the gap between research and clinical practice. In their article "The next generation of psychotherapy research: Reply to Ablon & Marci (2004), Goldfried and Eubanks-Carter (2004) and Haag (2004)" Western, Novotny, and Thompson-Brenner (2004b) sustain that, paradoxically, the focus on empirically supported therapies (ESTs) in clinical science has offered clinicians a limited view of what science has to offer psychotherapy.

Various researchers express concern about some of the limitations of RCT methods used to establish treatments as empirically supported, particularly regarding the balance between internal and external validity (Borkovec and Costonguay, 1998; Goldfried & Wolfe, 1996; Seligman, 1995).

Among the well-recognized technical limitations of the RCT paradigm are differential attrition, noncomparability of comparison groups, psychometric problems with outcome measures, inconsistency of treatment delivered, contamination by other treatments in trials of long-term therapy, and poor success in predicting outcomes at the level of individual cases from data summarized from group means (Margison et al., 2000).

In addition, a randomized clinical trial demands a treatment manual to assure fidelity and reliability of the intervention; however, everyday practice requires that the therapist constantly modify approaches to meet the idiopathic needs of the client. If the practitioner had to slavishly abide by the manual, this would lead to empathic failure and poor treatment for many patients (Levant, 2004). However, students are nowadays trained to adhere to the diagnostic manual that provides the proper procedure for treating a patient, most often using cognitive-behavioral therapy (CBT) or interpersonal psychotherapy (IPT), while they are taught to shun clinical hunches and predictions. For example, Wilson (1998) maintains that manual-based clinical work reflects statistical predictions, whereas divergence from manuals constitutes clinical predictions, but the latter should be avoided. Western, Novotny, and Thompson-Brenner (2004a) maintain that manuals are yet a very imperfect means of reflecting statistical prediction, since very few cases are atypical in clinical practice and that it is impossible to fully control the conditions of psychotherapy.

Even though "evidence-based practice" was a first step toward informed and empirically studied practice, we at CTS have resisted this approach, arguing for a more clinical and ecologically valid approach. The empirical validation of treatment models tends to remain firmly focused on the treatment outcomes and fails to consider important information regarding what is efficacious about a given treatment (Ablon and Marci, 2004; Goldfried & Eubanks-Carter, 2004). Arkowitz (1989) maintains that "basic psychopathology research on different clinical problems can reveal *what* needs to be changed, therapy process research can clarify *how* change occurs, and outcome research can specify *whether* change has occurred" (cited in Goldfried and Eubanks-Carter, 2004, p. 669). We believe that a research on psychotherapy should entail all three aspects.

To do so, research should be, first and foremost, carried out on everyday practice and not in artificially controlled settings with atypical patients (Ablon and Jones, 2002). While RCTs use randomization in the selection of subjects, clinical practice is not at all randomized. Randomization creates an artificial situation because it does not take into account the fact that patients actively choose their own treatment. Moreover, most patients used in control groups are volunteers, and this represents a significant methodology bias (Rapaport et al., 1996).

The RCT research paradigm, which is intended to inform clinical practice, assigns participants to treatments based solely on *DSM*-defined criteria, which is in turn based on a medical model and is not empirically well supported by psychotherapy research (Wampold, 2001). Even though the authors of *DSM IV* (APA, 1994) recognize that diagnosis does not necessary inform treatment. EST still follows these criteria in defining the problem and in evaluating improvement. As we saw earlier, we believe that therapists should make use of *operative descriptions* of the disorders, gathered from empirical research based on everyday practice. This also permits flexible adjustments in case of co-morbidity.[23] Our clinical

---

[23] We use the term "co-morbidity" to imply co-occurrence of more than one disorder.

experience teaches us that patients who come to therapy are not as diagnostically homogeneous as the patients used in RCTs. Meichenbaum (2003) reveals that fewer than 20 percent of mental-health patients have only one clearly definable Axis I diagnosis. Thus, the vast majority of cases seen by practitioners do not meet the exact criteria used in the RCTs. Various studies suggest that one-third of the patients who seek psychotherapeutic treatment, as a minimum, cannot be diagnosed according to DSM criteria because their problems either do not fit or else cross thresholds for any existing category (Howard et al., 1996; Messer, 2001; Western, Novotny, and Thompson-Brenner, 2004a; 2004 b).

We invite the reader to keep in mind that controlled clinical trials were initially designed by medical science so as to study the effectiveness of tested medications. A medical science would administer a specific medication and compare the results with a placebo or standard care condition. Unlike in medicine, in psychotherapy there is no counterpart to a placebo. Psychotherapy cannot be administered in such a pure form and adherence is much more difficult to measure (Ablon and Marci, 2004). Moreover, the nonspecific psychological treatments administered to patients in control groups are not "neutral" as in placebo medicine and they produce psychological effects regardless of whether these are clinically significant. In psychotherapy the social nature of the interaction is an important variable that RCTs fail to consider. We recognize that the EST approach did not give adequate weighting to extratherapeutic factors such as patients' expectancy, credibility of the treatment, waiting-list effects, and others that are inevitable and cannot be held constant. Ablon and Marci (2004) point out that treatment outcome cannot be predicted only from what the therapist does or, moreover, what the manual says the therapist should do, but from the emergent properties of the patient–therapy interaction. We are in total accordance with this notion. An analogy would be the fusion of the two gases, hydrogen and oxygen, whose end product is a totally different substance, a liquid, i.e. water.

We believe that a therapist should respond effectively to the particular needs and characteristics of the particular patient and his/her problematic situation, and that the model (comprising intervention strategies, communication, and relationship) the therapist chooses to follow should permit such flexibility and adaptability.

Western, Novotny, and Thompson-Brenner (2004a) argue that psychotherapy should return to the study of intervention strategies and of principles of change, which they consider a more useful means of analysis than the rigid treatment manuals that hold so many *a priori* decisions (length of interventions, timing of interventions, etc.). Once more, we accord with Western, Novotny, and Thompson-Brenner (2004a), who point out that therapists who follow mechanistic interventions to the letter, as dictated by manuals, can jeopardize therapy. We share their idea that therapists should, rather, hold guidelines to help keep a clear therapeutic focus.

RCTs make use of double-blind design of research. This design cannot be used in psychotherapy research, because patients cannot be blind as to what psychological treatment they are receiving since they actively participate in it; likewise, therapists cannot be kept blind because they have to know the treatment they are administering. RCTs make use of standardization-of-treatment procedures so that patients receive the same treatment. Once more, this is impossible to achieve in everyday psychotherapeutic practice. Even though different therapists practice the same techniques and procedures, treatment and outcomes are highly influenced by each therapist's personality and personal training. Furthermore, every encounter between a patient and a therapist is a unique event, which cannot be predicted or entirely standardized.

Another limitation of the ESTs approach is that it focuses on "efficacy" (internal validity) more than on "effectiveness" (high generalizability). In RCT there is a "trade-off" between rigor and generalizability (Shapiro et al., 1995). RCT samples are thoroughly selected and interventions are rigorously defined. This renders the treatment less applicable to routine practice (Margison et al., 2000).

The list of "well-established treatments" and "probably efficacious treatments" emphasized criteria that favored short-term behavioral and cognitive-behavioral approaches (Levant, 2004). This generated great regret and fury in practitioners who held other approaches. Chwalisz (2001) holds this responsible for the further inadequate clinical innovations, in both psychotherapy practice and research.

Duncan (2002), in accordance with Starcevic (2003), says that, "unlike the RCT, in actual clinical practice, manuals are not used, therapies are not ever purely practiced, clients are randomly assigned to treatments and clients rarely, if ever, enter therapy for singular DSM-defined disorders or experience success solely as diagnostic symptoms reduction" (p. 47). Thus, Duncan advised that, instead of assuming a medical model of psychotherapy, "a call is made for a systematic application of the common factors based on a relation model of client competence" (p. 32). This gave rise to the *common factor perspective*, which follows the "dodo bird verdict"[24] (Luborsky et al. 2002; Luborsky and Singer, 1975). This has become the metaphor to represent the state of psychotherapy outcome research (Luborsky et al., 2002; Luborsky & Singer, 1975). The most significant contribution about the common-factors approach was made by Lambert (1992), who, from his various reviews of outcome research, identified four therapeutic factors that obtain improvement in psychotherapy: extratherapeutic factors, common factors, expectancy or placebo, techniques. Lambert and Barley (2001) summarized this research literature: the therapy relationship and factors common to different therapies accounted for 30 percent; patient qualities and extratherapeutic change accounted for 40 percent; and expectancy and the placebo effect accounted for the remaining 15 percent; while specific techniques accounted for no more than 15 percent of the variance in therapy outcomes.

In our opinion, this study has managed to highlight the four main keys of practical work, but a shared criticism to this approach is related to the limited contribution attributed to the techniques in the explanation of improvement in psychotherapy (Castelnuovo, et al., 2004).

We believe that a specific technique characterizes and deeply influences the other three factors (Castelnuovo et al., 2004) and that all four factors are interrelated. Lambert and Barley (2001) show how most factors are related to the patient, his/her history, his/her expectation, and his/her resources. Thus the only thing that can be done to enhance therapy, or, better, the sole way

---

[24] The dodo bird verdict, based on Lewis Carol's novel *Alice's Adventures in Wonderland*, where at a point it is stated, "Everybody has won and all must have prizes."

clinicians can contribute to make their practice more efficacious and efficient, is to study their work so as to find innovative means to enhance their techniques, in such a way as to indirectly make use of, influence, and, when possible, increment the other three factors.

As has been shown throughout the book, we believe that a rigorous yet self-corrective model with a "flexible" intervention technique consequently supports the possibility of establishing an adequate therapeutic alliance, which in return can help support the patient's expectancy of the therapy and suggestibility (Nardone et al, 2000). The dialogue or interaction-communication technique used during the therapy, in order to be effective, should take account of and be tailored to the patient's qualities or resources, expectations, motivation/resistance, attempted solutions, and other extratherapeutic factors. Only in this way can the therapist emotionally overwhelm and mobilize the patient to move toward change (Nardone and Salvini, 2004). Jenkins (1996) notes that therapy should help by getting the client's own dialectical thinking capabilities operating again. Our experience leads us to assume that therapy should essentially mobilize the patient to *feel* the need to change (Nardone and Salvini, 2004).

Even the tasks or prescriptions given by the end of the session should be perceived as some sort of discovery made jointly by the therapist and the patient during their conversation, and these should take account of the patient's qualities (language, underlying logic, background, history of the disorder and previously attempted solutions, resistance to change, etc.) in order to increment the possibility of its being carried out.

Prochaska, di Clemente, and Norcross (1992) have intensively studied how individuals overcome their problems on their own. In support of the thesis, they assert, "in fact, it can be argued that all change is self-change, and that therapy is simply professionally coached self-change" (Prochaska, Norcross and Di Clemente, 1994, p. 17). We are in absolute accordance with this thesis. Norcross and Aboyoun, 1994) note that the persons who come to therapy are those who have failed in their self-change attempts. Once more, we are in line with this notion. We believe that clinicians should study the patient's failed attempted solutions and find effective means to unblock the "jammed system" and thus be able to use the patient's ability to generate change. Whether change begins before or during treatment, a crucial step of therapy is to use a specific technique that enhances as much as possible the effect of most factors so as to help clients work more effectively toward change, as well as its maintenance over time. Research findings show that change is more likely to be long-lasting in clients who attribute their changes to their own efforts (Lambert and Bergin, 1994) and clinicians should do what they can to confer this perception (Nardone and Salvini, 2004).

Regarding the placebo, our thesis is in line with Weil's (1995) concept of active placebo in medicine. Active placebos produce physiological changes and sensations, but do not bring about the actual healing (Tallman & Bohart, 1999). Healing takes place through the patient's self-healing, activated by the perceived bodily changes (Greenberg, 1999). Similarly, various techniques used in psychotherapy, are known to act as active placebos (Tallman and Bohart, 1999). Psychotherapeutic techniques seem not to be responsible for mediating change directly, but simply activate the natural healing propensity of the clients.

Tallman and Bohart say that the more active and specific a technique is, "the more believable it becomes to clients, thus mobilizing their intrinsic hope, energy, creativity, and self-healing potential. They claim that *"personal agency is awakened by technique"* (p. 101). They further assert that the "active placebo" process can offer a significant explanation of why techniques that evoke strong emotion may be particularly helpful, since they more effectively mobilize the client's involvement, commitment, and persistence toward self-change. We are in agreement with this theory and our efforts during these fifteen years of research and practice have been devoted to making our sessions as "mobilizing" as possible. In fact, one of our most advanced techniques is the strategic dialogue (discussed in Chapter 5), which aims at making the patient "feel" the need to involve himself in, commit himself to, and persist in following the indications given by the clinician, confident that these will lead him to change (Nardone and Salvini, 2004).

We obviously believe that a "good" therapeutic relationship is a fundamental component of change, which serves as a space for client's personal agency to flourish (Nardone, Milanese, Fiorenza, Mariotti, 2000). Clinical findings (Horvath, 1995; Orlinsky et al., 1994) reveal that the client's perceptions of the relationship or alliance correlate highly with therapeutic outcome. We believe that clinicians should provide the ideal relationship conditions for each individual patient, taking in consideration, once more, the type of problem, history of the disorder and attempted solutions, motivation/resistance, expectations, resources and other components, which all together determine the outcome of the therapy. Thus, the selected model should give the patient the idea of holding a leading role in the psychotherapeutic process and the merit of their improvement (Duncan, 2002; Duncan and Miller, 2000). Unfortunately, very few approaches or therapeutic models manage to convey this idea, primarily because they hold a deterministic epistemology. In this case the patient feels subjected to external factors such as drugs, "charisma" of the guru, expertise of therapist, and so forth (Castelnuovo et al., 2004).

Thus, even though we consider the common-factor perspective as having given us important knowledge about therapy, we believe that clinicians can play a much more active role in the therapeutic outcome. Practitioners should not rely on the "dodo verdict," which claims that all therapies are good, given that a large percentage of the therapeutic outcome depends entirely on the patient. Thus, this theory may lead one to assume that psychotherapy or psychological interventions can help only certain patients who have "favorable" extratherapeutic factors, high expectations and good relational skills, and are highly suggestible. We believe that it is the therapist who should have a "good" technique that can be tailored to the specific patient and therapeutic situation to maximize the possibility of change (Nardone and Watzlawick, 2004). Therapists or practitioners cannot rely on the notion that it is the "type" of patient (extratherapeutic factors, expectancy, motivation, suggestibility/placebo effect, etc.) that dictates whether the outcome of their work is positive or not.

Our clinical research and experience has revealed that a large percentage of patients who come or are forced into therapy cannot be described as fully collaborative or motivated to change. As we have already said in Chapter 4, we were able to distinguish four types of resistance/motivation toward change (Watzlawick and

Nardone, 1997; Nardone et al., 2000). We believe it is the prime responsibility of the therapist to identify the type of resistance and use adequate techniques to overcome it and thus help the patient move toward change. The premise of our work is that all patients could be helped to change; limits lie in the therapy and in the therapist. We believe that therapists should undergo continuous training so as to better their therapeutic interventions.

Even though we reaffirm that we hold therapeutic techniques as essential factors that deeply influence the functional accomplishment of other common factors, we acknowledge that these are far from being the *sole* factors that make therapy effective. In order to change a dysfunctional situation, the therapist should be able to establish a "good" therapeutic relationship, use adequate communication (direct or indirect language, unveiling and following the underlying logic, use of fitting aphorisms or other forms of reframing, one-down or one-up position, etc.) and tailor the entire therapy to the patient. This can be achieved only if the therapist holds a rigorous yet not rigid model. In our opinion, a "good" therapeutic model is not equivalent to a standardized manualized "package" but should require "adaptable" intervention, communication, and relationship techniques that can be also molded to the personal style of each individual therapist, thus allowing personal growth and evolution and improved therapeutic techniques and processes.

Moreover, treatment models and techniques need to evolve, because disorders are phenomena in continuous transition and evolution. In this discipline, maybe more than in others, since we work directly with human care and wellbeing, one should not allow one's achievements to become one's limits. We believe that a good clinician should be courageous enough not to sit on his laurels, but use his accomplishments to better his state of the art. As Leopardi said in his *Pensieri* (1995), "The most certain way to hide from others the limits of our knowledge is not to go beyond them."

Earlier in this chapter, we put forward the methodological bias present in EST studies, but various studies reveal that even the common-factors perspective holds significant methodological problems. One of the main research methods used in the common-factors perspective is the meta-analysis. Chambless (2002) was one

165

of the first to notice a number of significant problems within the meta-analysis of the effects of comparative psychotherapy studies led by Luborsky et al. (2002). Chambless disagrees with the opinion of Luborsky et al. that there lies no meaningful difference in the efficacy of various psychotherapies. Chambless bases his disagreement on the following grounds: (a) there seem to be significant errors in the data analysis; (b) research excludes certain clients such as children and adolescents; (c) erroneous generalizations have been made in the comparisons between therapies that have never been carried out; and (d) invalid assumptions that the average difference between all types of treatments for all kinds of problems can be assumed to represent the difference between any two types of treatment for a given problem. Chambless further maintains that "... concern for clients' welfare demands that psychologists be very wary of accepting the dodo bird verdict." Moreover, there are various studies that criticize meta-analysis, considering it an unsuitable methodological tool in the study of psychotherapy (Weiss and Weisz, 1990; Wilson and Lipsey, 2001). According to Shadish et al. (2000), "concern has arisen that meta-analysis overestimates the effects of psychological therapists and that those therapies may not work under clinically representative conditions" (p. 512).

Furthermore, the common-factors perspective focused its studies only on efficacy while giving no importance to efficiency. This perspective put all therapies on the same level regardless of the fact that some therapies take months to solve a problem while other therapies last years. And yet this aspect has great theoretical and social importance. In fact, there is quite a significant cost difference between the solution of a problem in three months and a solution in three years (Nardone and Watzlawick, 2004). The difference is in the cost, and this is not limited to a monetary value but above all in the fact that a person is going to lead a better life as soon as the problems that led him to therapy are solved. But oddly enough, as Garfield (1980) notes, what would seem to be a fundamental rule of professional ethics—the rapid solution of problems and suffering—has not been much considered by psychotherapists. Garfield explains this apparently incomprehensible attitude with the fact that for decades psychotherapeutic thought has been dominated by the idea that, to be effective, therapy must be prolonged, deep, and complex. However, this view, typical of traditional psychotherapeutic theories, has been decisively refuted by the research on the comparative efficacy of psychotherapy. In fact, various studies clearly demonstrate that there are no significant differences between results obtained in long-term therapy and those obtained in shorter therapy (Avnet, 1965; Bloom, 1995; Muench, 1965; Schlien, 1957; Luborsky, and Singer, 1975; Garfield, Prager, and Bergin, 1971; Butcher and Koss, 1978; Harris, Kalis, and Freeman, 1963, 1964; Phillips and Wiener, 1966; Gurman and Kniskern, 1978, Sirigatti 1994). In some cases, the research even indicated that shorter-term therapy was more effective (Bloom 1995; Nardone 1996). This position is confirmed by Assay and Lambert in their recent essay (1999):

> ... the beneficial effects of therapy can be achieved in short periods (5 to 10 sessions) with at least 50% of clients seen in routine clinical practice. For most clients, therapy will be Brief. This is not meant to be an endorsement of Brief therapy. It is simply a statement of fact. In consequence, therapists need to organize their work to optimize outcomes within a few sessions. Therapists also need to develop and practice intervention methods that assume clients will be in therapy for fewer than 10 sessions. A sizable minority of clients (20% to 30%) requires treatments lasting more than 25 sessions.

Adequate consideration of efficiency should be an important factor in the analysis and evaluation of the power of a therapeutic model. The time committed in obtaining results qualifies the result itself; in fact, the relation between therapy's costs and benefits will be more positive if treatment is less (Nardone and Watzlawick, 2004). Yet the common-factors prospective failed to take this in account.

Once more, we are back to the starting point, that is, the crucial role of research for "truly" improved practice. But again the dilemma remains: which is the most effective way in bridging research and practice?

A recent theory put together by Morrison and colleagues (2003) pinpoints two complementary possibilities in which clinical research can be carried out: one, by using efficacy trials and then test promising treatments in the laboratories using broader samples;

second, starting by using everyday clinical practice, in order to examine patterns of covariance between specific interventions and samples, so as to generate prototype treatments that can be used to guide future experimental studies.

In fact, contemporary methods of measurement seem to support "practice-based evidence," a complementary paradigm to improve clinical effectiveness in routine practice via the infra-structure of practice research networks (Margison et al., 2000). This involves collections of data from routine practice, allowing the practitioner to exercise clinical influence and an active role (ibid.). This approach suggests that outcome measurement should take in consideration improvement in wellbeing, symptoms and general life function respectively.

At the Centro di Terapia Strategica, research has been a funda-mental force in the evolution of brief strategic therapy throughout the entire fifteen years from its foundation, but our methodology goes beyond the "reductive" evidence-based model and the "diplomatic" common-factors perspective (Castlenuovo et al., 2004). Even though its design dates back more than a decade, it holds certain principles similar to the contemporary perspective that supports "practice-based evidence," even though there are some significant differences.

Our methodology

The action-research intervention approach

We concur on the notion that psychotherapy research should be carried out on everyday practice and should make use of only active treatments using assessment tools that should alter as little as possible the natural context of therapy. The research methodol-ogy used at our center, even though it cannot be defined as exper-imental, satisfies the criteria of an empirical approach (Meltzoff, 1998). The intent is not to systemically manipulate variables but to quantify the results of the therapeutic approach.

Since 1988, CTS has tried to enhance and develop the techniques and interventions following the action-research intervention approach.[25] Action-research methodologies aim to integrate action and reflection, so that the knowledge developed in the inquiry process is directly relevant to the issues being studied. Action research typically involves groups of participants and co-researchers and co-subjects engaging in cycles of action and critical reflection.

Reason and Bradbury (2001) describe action research as means that seeks to bring together action and reflection, theory and practice, in participation with others, in the pursuit of practical solutions to issues of pressing concern to people, and more generally the flourishing of individual persons and their communities.

This method led us to develop skills of reflective practice and a culture of inquiry as part of our work life. At the CTS this methodology helped us to simultaneously get to know a problematic situation, while introducing change, i.e. knowing through changing.

This allowed the significant reduction in the number of sessions necessary to overcome specific problems or disorders such as phobias, eating disorders, depression, and couple problems. This gave rise to the advanced model of brief strategic therapy.

Our research is based on the study of video/audio-taped sessions, which are then studied in detail by the associated researchers/therapists coming from different parts of Italy and European countries under the coordination of Professor Nardone. Our research entails the study of strategies related to the improvement of the technique, communication, and therapeutic relationship/alliance (Nardone, 1993; Nardone et al., 2000). Close examination of everyday practice led us to a better understanding of the studied disorders and to identify specific strategies related to the therapeutic

---

[25] "Action research" is a term used by Kurt Lewin (1951), meaning a compared analysis of conditions and effects of social actions that promote further social action. Action research has a long history, going back to social scientists' attempts to help solve practical problems in wartime situations in both Europe and America. Over the past ten years, there has been a resurgence of interest, and many developments in both theory and practice. The newer approaches to action research place emphasis on a full integration of action and reflection and on increased collaboration between all those involved in the inquiry project.

technique, communication, and relationship that led to more efficient and efficacious outcomes.

Our thesis lies on the belief that a problem can be understood and overcome only through empirical and experimental results, and not through mere observation that produces hypotheses based on *a priori* knowledge. The difference is between getting to know a problem through observation and getting to know a problem through change. Only in this way can we find efficient and efficacious techniques to provide help to those who need it.

Intervention protocols

We believe it is important to state that in these years our attempt has never been that of offering a rigid treatment "package," but to carry out research that can help reveal effective and efficacious intervention strategies that lead to change. Anticipating the suggestion by Western et al. (2004a) for better research and practice, our premise was always that of identifying specific treatment strategies or protocols rather than entire therapy manuals for each disorder or problem studied. We always considered this to be the sole functional means that can help therapists tailor their interventions to the particular patient and his/her problem.

The action-research intervention method helped us gather a more operative description of the disorders, which led us to progressively develop rigorous yet self-corrective strategic protocols for each specific disorder studied. The protocols are simple guidelines, which are far from being rigid and preordained. Protocols or strategic interventions are designed in a way that allows self-correction at any point in the therapy, since we are aware that the only way to really get to know a particular problem is through its solution. Thus, our protocols were subjected to various modifications and evolutions over the years; they are also continually subjected to modifications and adequate adjustments with each single case.

These protocols are highly replicable, predictable, and self-corrective. Through action research we were able to discover possible reactions to specific techniques (i.e. intervention, communication, and relationship) used, and thus we are now able to predict possible outcomes and then assign adequate tasks. Strategic protocols are predictable, because they are designed in a way that enables continuous verification of the obtained results. For example, action research has led us to predict four types of reaction to the paradoxical prescription, the so-called worst fantasy (see Chapter 6). Each step of the protocol is adjusted according to the patient's reaction to the specific technique. The techniques used during the session or prescribed at the end of the session, mobilize change but also help us therapists confirm or disconfirm the hypothesis made regarding the type of problem presented.

These protocols were not the product of spontaneous bursts of genius or great mastery, but of years of research based on everyday practice. As we have already declared in previous chapters, our first works were related to obsessive-phobic disorders but then our clinical studies embraced other issues such as eating disorders, child problems, family problems, obsessive-compulsive disorders, and depression, for which we have designed specific protocols. During this long-term experience, we have treated and studied hundreds and hundreds of patients coming from all over Italy and further afield. This confirmed the 'replicablility' of this method. Each specific protocol was applied to patients from different sociocultural backgrounds suffering from specific disorders, and the protocols were effectively applied not only by the great masters or gurus of this approach, but by various trained therapists with varying levels of clinical experience.

In addition, in the past ten years, scholars of the school not only "exported" and used these protocols in various regions of Italy, but also in other European countries and in the USA. Their contribution was fundamental in the gathering of good-quality data from routine practice, which helped render these protocols and the overtherapeutic techniques always more efficient and effective. In the past ten years, this collaboration developed into a sort of practice research network or inquiry community, where exchange of information and data is carried out periodically via the Internet and during our monthly meetings at Arezzo. We agree with Parry's (2000) promising vision of practice research networks. These can generate a great opportunity for bringing together clinicians who work in diverse fields and sociocultural backgrounds to pool data related to practice outcome, following the same set of measures in order to allow analysis of national or international datasets.

In 2003, following the First European Conference of Brief Strategic and Systemic Therapy organized in Arezzo, a European Network was officially set up to facilitate exchange of data, training, and comparisons between different therapies, and also between the different personal styles of therapists following the same model. Even though this network is still in the "newborn" phase, various collaborations have already taken off. These works will indubitably be the source of our next research-practice project.

Intervention and outcome measurement

Our work at CTS pivots on our conviction that there always exist improved means that can help us better our therapeutic interventions. But we strongly believe that this is possible only through ongoing experimental empirical research comprising formative and overall evaluation.

Formative evaluation is necessary because it is carried out while the process we wish to evaluate is still in progress. Its function is to verify internal effects and to see whether these are directed toward the objective established. For example, we verify the effects of the prescriptions from the changes reported by the patients, which the therapist will proceed to consolidate or to interrupt accordingly. This permits us to verify the efficacy of the strategies and to help us decide whether to proceed on this track or carry out eventual changes. This guarantees flexibility of the model.

Overall evaluation takes place once the process comes to an end. Its function is to verify whether the objective has been reached. In the last phase of therapy, this is carried out together with the patient, to evaluate the obtained results. This allows us to have a clearer picture of what took place and so lead to a further systemization of the model, favoring its diffusion. We believe that periodical follow-ups (three months, six months, one year) are necessary to verify that first-order change has taken place.

However, in order to measure improvement of each individual case while the client is still in therapy, we found very useful the use of the so-called "scale technique" (De Jong and Berg, 2001; Nardone, 1996; Nardone and Watzlawick, 1993, 2004) to detect the shared satisfaction of both therapist and patient about the clinical result. This technique is very simple to administer and consists of asking the patient to enumerate from 0 to 10 the results reached. We ask the patient the following question:

> If you had to give a mark to the improvement reached so far regarding your problem, 0 being the lowest, corresponding to when you came here asking us to help you with your problem, and 10 the maximum—when you will feel you can tell us, "Thank you, doctors, but I no longer need your help"—where do you place yourself now?

This gives the therapist clear data about the state of being and an opinion of the psychotherapy from the client's point of view (Nardone, 1996; Nardone and Watzlawick, 1993, 2004). We consider this measurement—even though it is not statistically precise and is highly subjective, affected by the patient's expectations, moods, skepticism, enthusiasm, and so forth—to be a functional means of helping us arrive at full recovery and resolution of a specific problem. Most often, the professional holds a different opinion of the improvement reached, but we believe that full recovery should be felt and expressed by the patient and not declared by clinician. In our opinion, psychological wellbeing is a subjective phenomenon and no scientifically precise measurement can persuade the patient that he is better or free from the presented problem if he is not experiencing this wellbeing in everyday life. The "scale technique" respects the patient's opinion and pace, while giving the therapist an indication of how to proceed.

In fact, this instrument becomes an extraordinary therapeutic strategy to take the patient beyond his/her present limitations. Whatever mark the patient gives himself, we invite him to fill in the missing steps to arrive at 10—the resolution of the presented problem. This method concretely evaluates what needs to take place to arrive at 10, but the process is carried out backwards, starting from 10, because this is the known shared goal, i.e. the resolution of the problem. Then we ask, "What needs to happen to feel at 9, what needs to happen to feel at 8, then 7 …?" and so forth. This technique is inspired by the mountain scouts, who plan their climb up the mountain in this way. Instead of planning their route from the bottom to the top of the mountain, they construct the route backwards, from its peak to its base, because this helps them avoid getting off track. Proceeding backwards makes it much easier to choose the best route, constructing its various phases, planning for intermediate stops and the possibility of changing routes if the climber encounters unexpected difficulties (Nardone et al., 2000). The same thing is carried out in therapy. We ask the patients to break up the remaining process into small steps, each corresponding to a specific sub-objective.

The logic behind this technique is to fragment something complicated into smaller goals in order to make it simple and manageable. Furthermore, this makes it possible to verify the effectiveness of the intervention at each stage, and correct it if the desired effects are not achieved. In other words, if an intervention is not working, the therapist can change his technique without jeopardizing the final result. Moreover, subdividing the objectives is a very good way of overcoming resistance to change. So that resistance is kept to a minimum, the intervention itself should also be minimal. The scale technique can be used together with the as-if technique to mobilize the patient to do something small and insignificant, yet sufficient to start a chain reaction capable of subverting the balance of the entire system (Thom, 1990). Thus, a small change is followed by a succession of small changes that will gradually lead to the big change—the resolution of the problem presented.

Moreover, when the patient finds himself having to fill in the missing steps to reach 10, he single-handedly comes to be aware that his present stand is not so distant from his full recovery and resolution of the problem and he autonomously comes to correct his rating on the scale.

Efficacy + efficiency = effectiveness

As illustrated throughout this book, the brief strategic approach is not concerned with a theory that can succinctly describe the concepts of normality and abnormality, nor with an all-embracing theory of "human nature." Rather, it is tied to the constructivist philosophy of knowledge, which is concerned with the appropriate means of making the individual's relationship with "reality" more functional. From such a theoretical perspective, the *efficacy of therapy* is represented by the *resolution of the patient's specific problem*.

The concept of "recovery" does not entail a complete absence of problems, but rather the overcoming of a specific problem experienced by the patient in a specific timeframe and context of his/her life. Therefore, the evaluation of the effects of strategic therapy can certainly be considered to be in agreement with the criteria stated above, with the caveat that no absolute generalization can be defined, and that success or the lack of it will be ascertained in relation to the initial therapeutic objectives. Accordingly, success will involve the solution of the patient's presenting problem and the achievement of goals that were agreed upon at the outset of therapy.

We consider a case resolved and the treatment completely successful only when the disappearance of symptoms and problems at the end of therapy is maintained over time, without relapses or substitution of new symptoms for the original ones. Thus, therapy is succeeded by three follow-up sessions, arranged for three months, six months, and one year after the end of treatment. The follow-up sessions are conducted as interviews directly with the patient and his family or partner. As an alternative, most therapists refer by phone (Talmon 1990; De Shazer, 1986; Geyerhofer, Komori 1997).

The efficacy of this type of treatment is clearly demonstrated in its high general success rate. The positive outcomes of treatment are 87 percent of the treated cases (Nardone and Watzlawick, 2004). In addition, this efficacy is even more evident in regard to specific problems, such as phobic disorders (agoraphobia and panic attacks), where there is a success rate of 95 percent (Nardone 1993; Nardone and Watzlawick, 2004). If we compare these data with the results of the research literature on the efficacy of different psychotherapeutic approaches (Andrews and Harvey, 1981; Bergin and Strupp, 1972; Garfield, 1981; Giles, 1983; Luborsky, Singer, and Luborsky, 1975; Sirigatti, 1988; Strupp and Hadley, 1979), which estimate the positive success rates of various therapies, according to the various approaches and research data, at 50–80 percent, it is obvious that the strategic approach has an efficacy superior to the other approaches. It also passed the follow-up test one year after the end of therapy.

The treatment efficacy of the strategic approach is maintained over time. The percentage of relapses is quite low, and the results obtained at the end of therapy are maintained in the majority of cases through the third follow-up—after one year—making future relapses or the emergence of substitute symptoms rather unlikely. In accord with Garfield (1980) and Assay and Lambert (1999), this refutes the supposition, common among a lot of therapists, that short-term therapies are superficial and lead inevitably to relapses into the original problem or to symptom displacement.

Treatment efficiency is the characteristic that, we believe, distinguishes the results of strategic therapy from those of other approaches.

Finally, if we consider the results obtained by the advanced model of brief strategic therapy when applied specifically to particular problems, as we have done in the past decade, not only in Italy but also in various European countries and in the USA, we see that both the efficacy and the efficiency of this approach have increased, compared with the already satisfactory results obtained by the previous general models. This increase in efficacy has been around 10 percent: from an average efficacy of 70 to 75 percent until the mid-eighties (Weakland et al., 1974; Koss, Butcher, and Strupp 1986; Gustafson, 1986; Gurman and Kniskern, 1986), to 80 to 86 percent in the past ten years (Monteczuma, 1996; Bloom 1997; De Shazer et al., 1986; Geyerhofer and Komori, 1995 ; Nardone and Watzlawick 1990; Nardone, 1996), with high points of efficacy reaching above 95 percent for particular forms of disorders (Madanes, 1990 and 1995; Nardone, 1996).

With the advanced model, in terms of efficiency, the number of sessions necessary to obtain the solution of the patient's presented problems has decreased to an average of five or six sessions (Bloom 1992; De Shazer, 1986; Geyerhofer and Komori, 1995 ; Nardone and Watzlawick, 1997; Nardone and Watzlawick, 2004;

Nardone, Milanese, and Verbitz, 1999), with the mobilizing of symptoms increasingly starting during the first few sessions, and often after the first session (Talmon, 1990; Bloom, 1995; Nardone, 1998; Nardone and Watzlawick, 2001). If we compare these results with those of different forms of evolved psychotherapy (Sirigatti 1988 and 1994; Assay and Lambert, 1999), we find that brief strategic approaches are unquestionably better-reaching more effective solutions to most mental and behavioral disorders at a lower cost; both financially and existentially.

The prospects for brief strategic therapy

As the reader has by now come to recognise from these pages, brief strategic therapy has undergone continuous growth and enhancement from its very origins, made possible by ongoing research and evaluation of the obtained results followed by subsequent modifications.

After the initial historical, almost "artistic" phase, in the sense that it was mainly founded on the genius-like intuitions of a few great therapists, brief therapy has thus become a rigorous model, based on continuous technical advancements developed from empirical clinical practice, action research, and the most advanced theoretical and epistemological formulations.

Our constant struggle is to work toward finding better means—in our strategies, communication, and therapeutic relationship—that take us beyond what has been achieved so far, and this can be done exclusively through systemic research on everyday practice. We are in accordance with Abrahamson's (2001) notion that practitioners should engage in a continuous search for evolved models that give equal weight to scientific rigor (i.e. treatment efficacy) and clinical utility (i.e. treatment effectiveness). That is our everyday "mission."

Our "mission" is to go beyond our present limits, and we are aware that this can be done through an always more appropriate integration of research and practice. We are conscious of the fact that we should not rest on our past achievements, but continuously look into and evaluate what has been achieved, to see a better future. As Eugene Delacroix (1961) says, "What moves men of genius, or rather what inspires their work, is not new ideas but their obsession with the idea that what had already been said is still not enough."

Bibliography

Ablon, J. S., and Jones, E. E. (2002), "Validity of controlled clinical trials of psychotherapy: Findings from the NIMH Treatment of Depression Collaborative Research Program", *American Journal of Psychiatry*, pp. 159, 775–83.

Ablon, J. S., and Marci, C. (2004), "Psychotherapy Process: The Missing Link: Comment on Western, Novotny, and Thompson-Brenner", *Psychological Bulletin*. 130 (4), pp. 664–8.

Abrahamson, D. J. (2001), "Treatment Efficacy and Clinical Utility: A Guidelines Model Applied to Psychotherapy Research", *Clinical Psychology: Science and Practice*, 8 (2), American Psychological Association.

Ackerman, N. W. (1958), *The Psychodynamics of Family Life: Diagnosis and Treatment of Family Relationships* (New York, NY: Basic Books).

Adams, R., and Victor, M. (1992), *Principles of Neurology* (New York: McGraw-Hill).

Alexander, F., and French, T. M. (1946), *Psychoanalytic Therapy* (New York, NY: Ronald Press).

American Psychiatric Association (APA) (1980), *Tardive Dyskinesia*, Task Force Report (Washington, DC: American Psychiatric Association).

American Psychiatric Association (APA) (1982), *Commission of Psychotherapies: Psychotherapy Research. Methodological and Efficacy Issues* (Washington, DC: American Psychiatric Association).

American Psychiatric Association (APA) (1987), *DSM III* (*Diagnostic and Statistical Manual of Mental Disorders III*) (Washington, DC: American Psychiatric Association).

American Psychiatric Association (APA) (1989), Task Force Report, *Treatments of Psychiatric Disorders* (4 vols) (Washington DC: American Psychiatric Association).

American Psychiatric Association (APA) (1990), Task Force Report, "Benzodiazepine Dependency, Toxicity, and Abuse" (Washington, DC: American Psychiatric Association).

American Psychiatric Association (APA) (1994), *DSM IV* (*Diagnostic and Statistical Manual of Mental Disorders IV*) (Washington, DC: American Psychiatric Association).

American Psychiatric Association (APA) Division of Clinical Psychology (1995), "Training in and dissemination of empirically validated psychological treatments: Report and recommendations", *Clinical Psychologist*, 48, pp. 3–27.

Amerio, P. (1982), *Teorie in psicologia sociale* (Bologna: Il Mulino).

Andrews, G., and Harvey, R. (1981), "Does Psychotherapy Benefit Neurotic Patients? A Reanalysis of the Smith, Glass and Miller Data", *Archives of General Psychiatry*, 38, pp. 1203–8.

Anonymous (1990), *I 36 stratagemmi: l'arte cinese di vincere* (Naples: Guida Editori).

Arcuri, L. (1994), "Giudizio e diagnosi clinica: analisi degli errori", *Scienze dell'Interazione*, 1 (1), pp. 107–16.

Arkowitz, H. (1989), "The role of theory in psychotherapy integration", *Journal of Integrative and Eclectic Psychotherapy*, 8, pp. 8–16.

Ashby, W. R. (1954), *Design for a Brain* (New York, NY: Wiley & Sons).

Ashby, W.R. (1956), *An Introduction to Cybernetics* (London: Methuen).

Assay, T. P, and Lambert, M. J. (1999), "The empirical case for the common factors in therapy: Qualitative findings", in M. A. Hubble, B. L. Duncan, and S. D. Miller (eds), *The Heart and Soul of Change: What works in therapy* (Washington, DC: American Psychological Association) pp. 33–56.

Austin, J. L. (1962), *How to Do Things with Words* (Cambridge, MA: Harvard University Press).

Avnet, H. H. (1965), "How Effective is Short-term Therapy?", in L. R. Wolberg (ed.), *Short-term Psychotherapy* (New York, NY: Grune and Stratton).

Bandler, R., and Grinder, J. (1975), *Patterns of the hypnotic techniques of Milton H. Erickson M.D.* (Palo Alto, CA: Meta Publications).

Bateson, G. (1967), "Cybernetic Explanation", *American Behavioral Scientist*, 10, pp. 29–32.

Bateson, G. (1972), *Steps to an Ecology of Mind* (New York, NY: Ballantine Books).

Bateson, G. (1980), *Mind and Nature* (New York, NY: Bantam Books).

Bateson, G., et al. (1956), "Toward a Theory of Schizophrenia", *Behavioral Science*, I, pp. 251–84.

Bell-Gadsby, C., and Siegenberg. A. (1996), *Reclaiming History: Ericksonian Solution-Focused Therapy for Sexual Abuse* (New York, NY: Brunner/Mazel Inc.).

Berg, I. K., and Dolan, Y. (2000), *Tales of Solution: A Collection of hope-inspiring stories* (New York, NY: W. W. Norton & Co.).

Berg, I. K., and Kelly, S. (2000), *Building Solutions in Child Protection Services* (New York, NY: W. W. Norton & Co.).

Berg, I. K., and Miller, S. (1992), *Working with the Problematic Drinker: A solution-focused approach* (New York, NY: W. W. Norton & Co.).

Bergin, A. E., and Lambert, M. J. (1978), "The Evaluation of Therapeutic Outcomes", in S. L. Garfield, A. E. Bergin (eds), *Handbook of Psychotherapy and Behavior Change* (New York, NY: Wiley & Sons).

Bergin, A. E., and Strupp, H. H. (1972), *Changing Frontiers in the Science of Psychotherapy* (Chicago, IL: Aldine).

Bertalanffy, L. von (1956), "General system theory", *General Systems Yearbook*, 1, pp. 1–10.

Bertalanffy, L. von (1962), "General system theory—A critical review", *General Systems Yearbook*, 7, pp. 1–20.

Birdwisthell, R. (1952), *Introduction to Kinetics* (Louisville, KY: University of Louisville Press).

Birdwisthell, R. (1970), *Kinesics and Context* (Harmondsworth, UK: Penguin).

Bloom, B. (1995), *Planned Short-Term Therapy* (Needham Heights, MA: Allyn & Bacon. Needham Heights.

Bloom, B. (1997), *Planned Short-term Psychotherapy: A clinical handbook*, 2nd edn (Boston, MA: Allyn & Bacon).

Borkovec, T. D., and Costonguay, L. G. (1998), "What is the scientific meaning of empirically supported therapy?", *Journal of Consulting and Critical Psychology*, 66 (1), pp. 136–42.

Borkovec, T. D., et al. (2001), "The Pennsylvania practice research network and future possibilities for clinically meaningful and scientifically rigorous psychotherapy effectiveness research", *Clinical Psychology: Science and Practice*, 8, pp. 155–67.

Butcher, J. N., and Koss, M. P. (1978), "M.M.P.I. Research on Brief and Crisis-Oriented Therapies", in S. L. Garfield, A. E. Bergin (eds), *Handbook of Psychotherapy and Behaviour Change*, 2nd edn (New York: Wiley & Sons).

Cade, B., and O'Hanlon, W. (1993), *A Brief Guide to Brief Therapy* (New York: W. W. Norton & Co.).

Castelnuovo, G., et al. (2004), "A critical review of Empirically Supported Treatments and Common Factors perspective in Psychotherapy", *Brief Strategic and Systemic Therapy: European Review*, Issue 1.

Chambless, D. L. (2002), "Beware the Dodo Bird: The Dangers of Overgeneralization", *Clinical Psychology: Science and Practice*, 9 (1).

Chambless, D., and Hollon, S. (1998), "Defining empirically supported therapies", *Journal of Consulting and Clinical Psychology*, 66, pp. 7–18.

Chwalisz, K. (2001), "A Common Factors Revolution: Let's Not 'Cut off Our Discipline's Nose to Spite its face' ", *Journal of Counseling Psychology*, 48 (3), pp. 262–7.

Cialdini R. B. (1984), *Influence: how and why people agree to things* (New York, NY: Morrow).

Cioran, E. (1993), *Sillogismi dell'amarezza* (Milan: Adelphi).

Da Costa, N. (1989a), "On the Logic of Belief", *Philosophical and Phenomenological Research*, 2.

Da Costa, N. (1989b), "The Logic of Self-Deception", *American Philosophical Quarterly*, 1.

De Jong, P., and Berg, I. K. (2001), *Interviewing for Solutions* (Stanford, CA: Wadsworth Publishing).

Delacroix, E. (1961), *The Journal of Eugene Delacroix* translated from French by Walter Pach (New York, Grove press)

Depolo M., and Sarchielli G. (1991), *Psicologia dell'organizzazione* (Bologna: Il Mulino).

De Shazer, S. (1982), *Patterns of Brief Family Therapy* (New York, NY: Guilford).

De Shazer, S. (1985), *Keys to Solution in Brief Therapy* (New York, NY: W.W. Norton and Co.).

De Shazer, S. (1988), *Clues: Investigating Solutions in Brief Therapy* (New York, NY: W. W. Norton & Co.).

De Shazer, S. (1991) *Putting Difference to Work* (New York, NY: W.W. Norton and Co.).

De Shazer, S., et al. (1986), "Brief Therapy: Focused solution development", *Family Process*, 25, pp. 207–22.

Di Stefano, G. (1986), *Sistemi di gestione strategica aziendale*, 2nd edn, (Milan: Angeli).

Doise, W. (1973), "Relations et représentasions intergroups", in S. Moscovici (ed.), *Introduction à la psychologie sociale* (Paris: Larousse).

Doise, W. (1978), "Images, représentasions, idéologies et expérimentation psychosociologique", *Social Science Information*, 17.

Dolan, Y. (1998), *One Small Step: Moving beyond trauma and therapy to a life of joy* (Watsonville, CA: Papier-Mâché Press).

Doyle, A. C. (1995), *Gli aforismi di Sherlock Holmes* (Rome: Newton Compton).

Duncan, B. L. (2002), "The Legacy of Saul Rosenzweig: The Profundity of the Dodo Bird", *Journal of Psychotherapy Integration*, 12 (1), pp. 32–57.

Duncan, B. L., Hubble, M. A., and Miller, S. D. (1997a), *Psychotherapy with "Impossible" Cases: The Efficient treatment of therapy veterans* (New York: W. W. Norton & Co.).

Duncan, B. L., Hubble, M. A., and Miller, S. D. (1997b), "Stepping off the throne", *Family Therapy Networker*, 21 (4), pp. 22–31, 33.

Duncan, B. L., and Miller, S. D. (2000), *The Heroic Change: Doing client-directed outcome-informed therapy* (San Francisco, CA: Jossey-Bass Inc.).

Ekman, P. (1985), *Telling Lies*, New York, London: W. W. Norton & Co.).

Ekman, P., and Friesen, W. V. (1975), *Unmasking the Face* (Englewood Cliffs, N.J.: Prentice-Hall).

Elliott, R. (1998), "Editor's introduction: a guide to the empirically supported treatments controversy", *Psychotherapy Research*, 8, pp. 115–25.

Elster, J. (1979), *Ulysses and the Sirens* (Cambridge, UK: Cambridge University Press).

Elster, J. (ed.) (1985), *The Multiple Self* (Cambridge, UK: Cambridge University Press).

Erickson, M. H., and Rossi, E. L. (1979), *Hypnotherapy: An Exploratory Casebook* (New York, NY: Irvington).

Erickson, M. H., and Rossi, E. L. (eds) (1980), *The Collected Papers of Milton H. Erickson on Hypnosis*, Vols I, II, III, IV (New York, NY: Irvington).

Fiora, E., Pedrabissi, L., and Salvini, A. (1988), *Pluralismo teorico e pragmatismo conoscitivo in psicologia della personalità* (Milan: Giuffrè).

Fiorenza, A. (2000), *Bambini e ragazzi difficili: Figli che crescono: soluzioni a problemi che emergono. Terapia in tempi brevi* (Milan: Ponte alle Grazie).

Fiorenza, A., and Nardone, G. (1995), *L'intervento strategico nei contesti educativi* (Milan: Giuffré).

Fisch, R., Weakland, J. H., and Segal, L. (1982), *The Tactics of Change: Doing therapy briefly* (San Francisco, CA: Jossey-Bass Inc.).

Foerster, H. von (1973), "On Constructing a Reality", in W. F. E. Preiser (ed.), *Environmental Design Research*, Vol. 2, (Stroudsburg: Dowden, Hutchinson & Ross), pp. 35–46.

Foerster, H. von (1987), *Sistemi che osservano* (Rome: Astrolabio).

Frank, J. D. (1973), *Persuasion and Healing: A comparative study of psychotherapy* (Baltimore, MD: Johns Hopkins University Press).

Frank, J. I. (1971), "Therapeutic Components of Psychotherapy. A 25 Year Progress Report of Research", *Journal of Consulting and Clinical Psychology*, 37, pp. 307–13.

Garfield, S. L. (1980), *Psychotherapy and the Eclectic Approach* (New York, NY: Wiley & Sons).

Garfield, S. L. (1981), "Psychotherapy. A 40 Year Appraisal", *American Psychologist*, 2, pp. 174–83.

Garfield, S. L. (1989), *The Practice of Brief Psychotherapy* (New York, NY: Pergamon Press).

Garfield, S. L., and Bergin, A. E. (1986), "Evaluation and Outcome in Psychotherapy", in S. L. Garfield, A. E. Bergin (eds), *Handbook of Psychotherapy and Behavior Change* (New York, NY: Wiley & Sons).

Garfield, S. L., Prager, R. A., and Bergin, A. E. (1971), "Evaluation of outcome in psychotherapy", *Journal of Consulting and Clinical Psychology*, 37 (3) pp. 307–13.

Geyerhofer, S., and Komori, Y. (1997), "Integrazione di modelli post-strutturalisti di terapia breve", in Watzlawick P., and Nardone, G. (eds), *Terapia Breve Strategic* (Milan; Raffaello Cortina Editore).

Giles, T. R. (1983), "Probable Superiority of Behavioral Interventions: I, Traditional Comparative Outcome", *Journal of Behavior Therapy and Experimental Psychiatry*, 14 (1), pp. 29–32.

Gladwell, M. (2000), Il punto critico (Milan: Rizzoli).

Glasersfeld, E. von (1984), "An introduction to radical constructivism", in P. Watzlawick (ed.), *The Invented Reality* (New York, NY: W. W. Norton & Co.).

Glasersfeld, E. von (1995), *Radical Constructivism* (London: The Falmer Press).

Gödel, K. (1931), "Ueber formal unentscheidbare Sätze del Principia Matematica und verwandter Systeme", *Monatshefte für Mathematik und physik*, 38, pp. 173–98.

Goethe, J. W. (1983), *Massime e riflessioni* (Rome: Theoria).

Goldfried, M. R., and Eubanks-Carter, C. (2004), "On the need for a new psychotherapy research paradigm: Comment on Western, Novotny and Thompson-Brenner", *Psychological Bulletin*, 130, pp. 669–73.

Goldfried, M. R., and Wolfe, B. E. (1996), "Psychotherapy practice and research: Repairing a strained alliance", *American Psychologist*, 51, pp. 1007–16.

Grana, N. (1990), *Contraddizione e incompletezza* (Naples: Liguori).

Greenberg, L. S. (1999), "Common Psychosocial Factors in Psychiatric Drug Therapy", in M. A., Hubble, B. L., Duncan and S. C., Miller, *The Heart & Soul of Change: What works in Therapy* (1999) pp. 91–131 (Washington, DC: American Psychological Association).

Gurman, A. S., and Kniskern, D. P. (1978), "Research on marital and family therapy", in S. L. Garfield and A. E. Bergin (eds), *Handbook of Psychotherapy and Behaviour Change*, 2nd edn (New York, NY: Wiley & Sons).

Gurman, A. S., and Kniskern, D. P. (1986), "Research on Marital and Family Therapy", in S. L. Garfield, A. E. Bergin (eds), *Handbook of*

Psychotherapy and Behavior Change, 2nd edn (New York, NY: Wiley & Sons).

Gustafson, J. P. (1986), *The Complex Secret of Brief Psychotherapy* (New York: W. W. Norton & Co.).

Haley, J. (1963), *Strategies of Psychotherapy* (New York, NY: Grune & Stratton).

Haley, J. (1973), *Uncommon Therapy: The Psychiatric Techniques of M. Erickson, M.D.* (New York: W.W. Norton & Co).

Haley, J. (1976), *Problem-Solving Therapy* (San Francisco, CA: Jossey-Bass Inc.).

Hall, E. T. (1966), *The Hidden Dimension* New York, NY: Doubleday).

Harris, M. R., Kalis, B., and Freeman, E. H. (1963), "Precipitating Stress: an Approach to Brief Therapy", in *American Journal of Psychotherapy*, 17, pp. 465–71.

Harris, M. R., Kalis, B., and Freeman, E. H. (1964), "An Approach to Short-Term Psychotherapy", *Mind*, 8, pp. 198–206.

Heisenberg, W. (1958), *Physics and Philosophy* (New York, NY: Harper).

Henry, W. P. (1998), "Science, politics and the politics of science: the use and misuse of empirically validated treatment research", *Psychotherapy Research*, 8, pp. 126–40.

Herbert, J. D. (2003), "The science and practice of empirically supported treatments", *Behavior Modification*, 27 (3), pp. 412–30.

Hobbes, T. (1969), *Behemoth, or the Long Parliament*, 2nd edition (London: Cass).

Hoffman, L. (1981), *Foundations of Family Therapy* (New York, NY: Basic Books).

Horvath, A. O. (1995), The therapeutic relationship: From transference to alliance. *In Session*. 1, pp. 7–17.

Howard, K. I., et al. (1996), "Evaluation of psychotherapy: Efficacy, effectiveness and patient progress", *American Psychologist*, 51, pp. 1059–64.

Hubble, M. A., Duncan, B. L., and Miller S. C. (eds), (1999), *The Heart & Soul of Change: What works in Therapy* (Washington, DC: American Psychological Association).

Ippocrate, (1991), Hersant, Y. (ed), *Sul riso e le follia* (Palermo: Sellerio Editore).

Jenkins, A. H. (1996), "Enhancing the patient's dialectical abilities in psychotherapy", paper presented at the 104th annual symposium on "How Clients Create Change in Psychotherapy: Implications for Understanding Change", Convention of the American Psychological Association, Toronto.

Jullien, F. (1996), *Traité de l'efficacité* (Paris: Grasset & Fasquelle).

Kelly, G. A. (1955), *The Psychology of Personal Constructs* (2 vols) (New York: W. W. Norton & Co.).

Koocher. G. (2003), personal communication cited in R. F. Levant, "The Empirically Validated Treatments Movement: A Practitioner/educator Perspective", *Clinical Psychology: Science and Practice*. Vol. 11, No. 2.

Koss, M. P., Butcher, J. N., and Strupp, H. H. (1986), "Brief psychotherapy methods in clinical research". *Journal of Consulting & Clinical Psychology*, 54 (1), pp. 60–7.

Labroit, H. (1982), *L'elogio della fuga* (Milan: Mondadori).

Lambert, M. J. (1992), "Implications of outcome research for psychotherapy integration", in C. Norcross and M. R. Goldfried (eds), *Handbook of Psychotherapy Integration* (New York: Basic Books), pp. 94–129.

Lambert, M. J., and Barley, D. E. (2001), "Research summary on the therapeutic relationship and psychotherapy outcome", *Psychotherapy: Theory, Research, Practice, Training.*, 38, pp. 357–61.

Lambert, M. J., Bergin, A. E. (1994), "The effectiveness of psychotherapy", in A. E. Bergin and S. L. Bellack (eds), *Issues in Psychotherapy Research* (New York: Plenum Press), pp. 313–59.

Lazarus, A. A. (1981), *The Practice of Multimodal Therapy* (Baltimore, MD: Johns Hopkins University Press).

Le Bon, G. (1895), *La psychologie des foules* (Paris: PUF), new edn, 1963.

Leopardi, G. (1995), Salvarezza, M., (ed.) *Pensieri* (Milan; Biblioteca Italiana Tascabile).

Levant, R. F. (2004), "The Empirically Validated Treatments Movement: A Practitioner/educator Perspective", *Clinical Psychology: Science and Practice*, Vol. 11, No. 2.

Lewin, K. (1951), *Field Theory in Social Science: selected theoretical papers*, ed. D. Cartwright (New York, NY: Harper & Row).

Leyens, J. P. (1983), *Somme-nous tous des psychologues?*, (Brussels; Pierre Mardaga).

Lichtenberg, C. G. (1978), *Das Lichtenberg trost Büchlein* (Munich: Meyster Verlag).

Luborsky, L., and Singer, B. (1975), Comparative studies of psychotherapies. Is it true that "everyone has one and all must have prizes"? *Archives of General Psychiatry, 32*(8), pp. 995–1008.

Luborsky, L., et al. (2002), "The dodo bird verdict is alive and well— mostly", *Clinical Psychology: Science and Practice*, 9 (1), pp. 2–12.

Madanes, C. (1990), *Behind the One-Way Mirror* (San Francisco, CA: Jossey-Bass Inc.).

Madanes, C. (1995), *The Violence of Man* (San Francisco, CA: Jossey-Bass Inc.).

Mandel, G. (ed.) (1994), *Budda Breviario* (Milan: Rusconi).

Margison, F. R., et al., (2000), "Measurement and psychotherapy: Evidence-based practice and practice-based medicine", *British Journal of Psychiatry* 177, pp. 123–30.

Maturana, H. R., and Varela, F. J. (1980), *Autopoiesis and Cognition: The realization of the living* (Dordrecht, Holland: Reidel).

Meichenbaum, D. (2003), "Treating Individuals with angry and aggressive behaviours: A life-span Cultural Perspective", paper presented at the annual meeting of the Georgia Psychological Association, Atlanta, GA.

Meltzoff, J. (1998), *Critical Thinking about Research* (Washington, DC: American Psychiatric Association).

Messer, S. (2001) "Empirically supported treatments: What's a non-behaviourist to do?", in B. D. Slife, R. N. Williams, and D. Barlow (eds), *Critical Issues in Psychotherapy: Translating new ideas into practice* (Thousand Oaks, CA: Sage Publications), pp. 3–19.

Monteczuma, C. (1996), Personal communication and presentation at the "Global reach of Brief Strategic Therapy" conference, Vienna, June 1996.

Morris, D. (1977), *Manwatching: A Field Guide to Human Behaviour* (Oxford: Equinox).

Morris, D. (1995), *I gesti nel mondo* (Milan: Mondadori).

Morrison, K. H., Bradley, R., and Western, D. (2003), "The external validity of controlled clinical trials of psychotherapy for depression and anxiety: a naturalistic study", *Psychology and Psychotherapy*, 76 (Pt 2), pp. 109–32.

Moscovici, S. (1967), "Communication processes and properties of language", in L. Berkowitz (ed.), *Advances in Experimental Social Psychology*, Vol. III (New York, NY: Academic Press), pp. 225–70.

Moscovici, S. (1972), *The Psychosociology of Language* (Chicago, IL: Markham).

Moscovici, S. (1976), *Social Influence and Social Change* (New York, NY: Academic Press).

Muench, G. A. (1965), "An Investigation of the Efficacy of Time-limited Psychotherapy", *Journal of Counselling Psychology*, 12, pp. 294–9.

Nardone, G. (ed.) (1988), *Modelli di psicoterapia a confronto* (Rome: Il Ventaglio).

Nardone, G. (1991), *Suggestione ° Ristrutturazione = Cambiamento. L'approccio strategico e costruttivista alla psicoterapia breve* (Milan: Giuffrè).

Nardone, G. (1993), *Paura, Panico, Fobie* (Milan: Ponte alle Grazie) (En. tr., 1996, *Brief Strategic Solution-Oriented Therapy of Phobic and Obsessive Disorders* (Northvale, NJ: Jason Aronson, Inc.)). French Edition, 1996, *Peur, Panique, Phobies* (Bordeaux: L'Esprit du Temps). Spanish Edition, 1995, *Miedo, Panico, Fobias* (Barcelona: Editorial Herder). German Edition, 1997, *Systemisch Kurztherapie bei Zwängen und Phobien* (Bern: Verlag Hans Huber).

Nardone, G. (1994), "La Prescrizione Medica. Strategia di comunicazione ingiuntiva", in *Scienza dell'Interazione*, 1, pp. 81–90.

Nardone, G. (1994a), *Manuale di sopravvivenza per psicopazienti* (Firenze: Ponte alle Grazie).

Nardone, G. (1994b), "La prescrizione medica: strategie di comunicazione ingiuntiva", *Scienze dell'Interazione*, 1 (1), pp. 81–90.

Nardone, G. (1995a), "Brief strategic therapy of phobic disorders: A model of therapy and evaluation research", in J. H. Weakland and W. A. Ray (eds), *Propagations: thirty years of influence from the Mental Research Institute* (New York, NY: Haworth Press Inc.).

Nardone, G. (1995b), "Conoscere un problema mediante la sua soluzione: i sistemi percettivo-reattivi patogeni e la psicoterapia strategica", in G. Pagliaro, M. Cesa-Bianchi (*a cura di*), Nuove prospettive in psicoterapia e modelli interattivo-cognitivi, Angeli, Milano.

Nardone, G. (1996), *Brief Strategic Solution-oriented Therapy of Phobic and Obsessive Disorders* (Northvale, NJ: Jason Aronson, Inc.).

Nardone, G. (1998), *Psicosoluzioni* (Milan: Rizzoli).

Nardone, G. (2000), *Oltre il limiti della paura* (Milan: Rizzoli).

Nardone, G. (2003), *Cavalcare la propria tigre: Gli stratagemmi nelle arti marziali ovvero come risolvere problemi difficili attraverso soluzioni templi* (Milan: Ponte alle Grazie).

Nardone, G., et al. (2000), *La terapia dell'azienda malata: problem solving strategico per organizzazioni* (Milan: Ponte alle Grazie).

Nardone, G., and Portelli, C. (2005), "When the diagnosis invents the illness", *Kybernetes: The International Journal of Systems & Cybernatics*, Vol. 34, No. 3–4, pp. 365–72, Emerald Group Publishing Limited, Bradford, UK.

Nardone. G., Rocchi, R., and Giannotti, E. (2001) *Modelli di Famiglia. Conoscere e risolvere i problemi tra genitori e figli* (Milan: Ponte alle Grazie). Spanish Edition, 2003, *Modelos de familia* (Barcelona: Editorial Herder).

Nardone, G., and Salvini, A. (1997), "Logica matematica e logiche non ordinarie come guida per il problem-solving strategico", in P. Watzlawick, G. Nardone (editors) *Terapia breve strategica* (Milan: Raffaello Cortina Editore), pp. 53–61.

Nardone, G., and Salvini, A. (2004), *Il Dialogo Strategico: Comunicare persuadendo: tecniche evolute per il cambiamento* (Milan: Ponte alle Grazie).

Nardone, G., Verbitz, T., and Milanese, R. (1999), *Le prigioni del cibo. Vomiting, Bulimia, Anoressia: la terapia in tempi brevi* (Firenze: Ponte alle Grazie). Spanish Edition, 2002, *Las prisiones de la comida* (Barcelona: Editorial Herder). German Edition, 2003, *Systemisch Kurztherapie bei Ess-Störungen* (Bern: Verlag Hans Huber). French Edition, 2004, *Manger beaucoup, à la folie, pas du tout* (Paris: Editions du Seuil). British Edition (in press), *The Prisons of Food: Strategic Solution-oriented Research and Treatment of Eating Disorders* (London: Karnac Publishing).

Nardone, G., and Watzlawick, P. (1990), *L'Arte del Cambiamento: manuale di terapia strategica e ipnoterapia senza trance* (Milan: Ponte alle Grazie).

Nardone, G., and Watzlawick, P. (1993), *The Art of Change: Strategic Therapy and Hypnotherapy Without Trance* (San Francisco, CA: Jossey-Bass Inc.).

Nardone, G., and Watzlawick, P. (eds) (2004), *Brief Strategic Therapy: Philosophy, Technique and Research*. (Maryland, USA: Rowman & Littlefield Publishers, Aronson Group).

Neumann, J. von, and Morgenstern, O. (1944), *Theory of Games and Economic Behaviour* (Princeton, NJ: Princeton University Press).

Norcross, J. C., and Aboyoun, D. C. (1994), "Self-change experiences of psychotherapists", in T. M. Brinthaupt and R. P. Lipka (eds), *Changing the Self* Albany, NY: State University of New York Press), pp. 253–78.

Omer, H. (1992), "From the one truth to the infinity of constructed ones", *Psychotherapy*, 29, pp. 253–61.

Omer, H. (1994), *Critical Interventions in Psychotherapy* (New York, NY: W. W. Norton & Co.).

Orlinsky, D. E., Grawe, K., and Parks, B. K. (1994), "Process and outcome in psychotherapy—Nocheinmal", in A. E. Bergin and S. L. Garfield (eds), *Handbook of Psychotherapy and Behavior Change*, 4th edn (New York, NY: John Wiley & Sons), pp. 270–378).

Orstein, R. (1986), *Multimind* (Boston, MA: Author Book).

Paguni, R. (1991), *La ricerca in psicoterapia* (Rome: Armando).

Parry, G. (2000), "Evidence-based psychotherapy: special case or special pleading?", *Evidence-Based Mental Health*, 3, pp. 35–7.

Pascal, B. (1995) A.J. Krailsheimer (translator) Penées (USA; Penguin Classics) Italian version (1962), *Pensieri* (Turin: Einaudi).

Patterson, M. L. (1982), "A sequential functional model of non verbal exchange", *Psychological Review*, 19 (3), pp. 231–49.

Pera, M. (1991), *Scienza e retorica* (Bari: Laterza).

Peters, T. (1997), *Wow! Un successo da urlo* (Milan: Sperling & Kupfer).

Phillips, D. (1972), *Metodologia della ricerca* (Bologna: Il Mulino).

Phillips, D. (1974), "The Influence of Suggestion on Suicide: Substantive and Theoretical Implications of the Werther Effect, *American Sociological Review*, 39, pp. 340–54.

Phillips, D. (1979), "Suicide, Motor Vehicle Fatalities, and the Mass Media: Evidence Toward a Theory of Suggestion", *American Journal of Sociology*, 84, pp. 1102–14.

Phillips, D. (1980), "Airplane Accident, Murder and the Mass Media: Toward a Theory of Imitation and Suggestion", *Social Forces*, 58, pp. 1001–24.

Philips, E. L., and Weiner, D. N. (1966), *Short-Term Psychotherapy and Structural Behaviour Change* (New York, NY: McGraw-Hill).

Piagliaro, G. (1995), "Nuove Prospettive", in M. Case Bianchi (ed.), *Psicoterapia e Modelli Interattivo-Cognitivo* (Milan: Franco Angeli).

Popper, K. R. (1972), *Objective Knowledge* (London: Oxford University Press).

Popper, K. R. (1976), *Congetture e confutazioni* (Bologna: Il Mulino).

Popper, K. R. (1983), *Realism and the Aim of Science* (London: Hutchinson).

Popper, K. R. (1998), *Breviario* (Milan: Rusconi).

Portelli, C. (2004), "Advanced Brief Strategic Therapy for Obsessive-Compulsive Disorder", *Brief Strategic & Systemic Therapy: European Review*, Issue 1.

Price, J. A. (1996), *Power & Compassion: Working with difficult adolescents & abused parents* (New York, NY: W. W. Norton & Co.).

Prochaska, J. O., Di Clemente, C. C., and Norcross, J. C., (1992), "In search of how people change: Application to additive behaviours". *American Psychologists*, 47, pp. 1102–14.

Prochaska, J. O., Di Clemente, C. C., and Norcross, J. C., (1994) *Changing for Good* (New York, NY: Morrow).

Rabkin, R. (1977) *Strategic Psychotherapy* (New York, NY: Basic Books).

Rapaport, M. H., et al. (1996), "A comparison of descriptive variables for clinical patients and symptomatic volunteers with depressive disorders", *Journal of Clinical Psychopharmacology*, 16 (3), pp. 242–6.

Reason, P., and Bradbury, H. (2001), *Handbook of Action Research* (Thousand Oaks, CA: Sage Publications).

Ricci Bitti, P. E., and Zani, B (1983), *La comunicazione come processo sociale* (Bologna: Il Mulino).

Romano, D. F., and Felicioli R. P. (1992), *Comunicazione interna e processo organizzativo* (Milan: Raffaello Cortina Editore).

Rosenhan, D. (1990), "Essere sani in posti insani", in P. Watzlawick (ed.), *La realtà inventata* (Milan: Feltrinelli).

Rosenthal, R., and Jacobson, L. (1968), *Pygmalion in the Classroom: teacher expectation and pupil's intellectual development* (New York, NY: Rinehart & Winston, Holt).

Salvini, A. (1988), "Pluralismo teorico e pragmatismo conoscitivo: assunti metateorici in psicologia della personalità", in E. Fiora, I. Pedrabissi, and A. Salvini, *Pluralismo teorico e pragmatismo conoscitivo in psicologia della personalità* (Milan: Giuffrè).

Salvini, A. (1995), "Gli schemi di tipizzazione della personalità in psicologia clinica e psicoterapia", in G. Pagliaro and M. Cesa-Bianchi (*a cura di*), *Nuove prospettive in psicoterapia e modelli interattivo-cognitivi* (Milan: Angeli).

Sanderson, W. C. (2003), "Why empirically supported psychological treatments are important". *Behavior Modification*, 27 (3), pp. 290–9.

Schlein, E. H. (1987), *Process Consultation* (Boston, USA: Addison-Wesley Publishing Company Inc.).

Schrödinger, E. (1958), *Mind and Matter* (Cambridge, UK: Cambridge University Press).

Seligman, M. E. P. (1995), "The effectiveness of psychotherapy: The Consumer Reports survey", *American Psychologist*, 50, 965–74.

Selvini Palazzoli, M. (1963), *L'Anoressia Mentale* (Milan: Feltrinelli).

Selvini Palazzoli, M., et al. (1975), *Paradosso e controparadosso* (Milan: Feltrinelli).

Selvini Palazzoli, M., et al. (1988), *I giochi psicotici nella Famiglia* (Milan: Raffaello Cortina Editore).

Shadish, W. R., et al. (2000) "The effects of psychological therapies under clinically representatives conditions: a meta-analysis" *Psychological Bulletin*, 126 (4), pp. 512–29.

Shapiro, D.A., et al. (1995), "Decisions, decisions: Determining the effect of treatment method and duration on the outcome of psychotherapy for depression", in M. Avelline and D. A. Shapiro (eds), *Research Foundations for Psychotherapy Practice* (Chichester: Wiley & Sons), pp. 151–74.

Schlien, J. M. (1957), "Time-limited psychotherapy: an experimental investigation of practical values and theoretical implications", *Journal of Counselling Psychology*, 4, pp. 318–29.

Sirigatti, S. (1975), "Behaviour Therapy and Therapist Variables: A–B Distinction in the Treatment of Monophobias" *Bollettino di psicologia applicata*, pp. 127–9.

Sirigatti, S. (1988), "La ricerca valutativa in psicoterapia: modelli e prospettive", in G. Nardone (ed.), *Modelli di psicoterapia a confronto* (Rome: Il Ventaglio).

Sirigatti, S. (1994), "La ricerca sui processi e i risultati della psicoterapia", *Scienze dell'interazione* 1 (Firenze: Pontecorboli).

Skorjanec, B. (2000), *Il linguaggio della terapia breve* (Firenze: Ponte alle Grazie).

Sluzki, C. E., and Ransom, D. C. (1976), *Double Bind* (New York, NY: Grune & Stratton).

Sluzki, C. E., and Ransom, D. C. (1979), *Double Bind: The Foundation of the Communicational Approach to the Family* (New York: Grune and Stratton).

Starcevic, V. (2003), "Psychotherapy in the era of evidence-based medicine", *Australian Psychiatry*, 11 (3), pp. 278–81.

Stolzenberg, G. (1978), "Can an inquiry into the foundations of mathematics tell us anything interesting about mind?", in Miller, G.A., Lennenberg, E., (eds) *Psychology and Biology of Language and Thought* (New York, NY: Academic Press).

Stonich, P. J. (1985), *Strategia in azione* (Turin: ISEDI).

Strupp, H. H., and Hadley, S. W. (1979), "Specific vs. Nonspecific Factors in Psychotherapy: a Controlled Study of Outcome", in *Archives of General Psychiatry*, 36, pp. 1125–36.

Tallman, K., and Bohart, A. C. (1999), "The Client as a Common Factor: Clients as Self-Healers", in M. A., Hubble, B. L., Duncan, and S. D. Miller (eds), *The Heart & Soul of Change: What Works in Therapy* (Washington, DC: American Psychological Association), pp. 91–131.

Talmon M. (1990), *Single Session Therapy* (San Francisco, CA: Jossey-Bass Inc.).

Tarde G. (1901), *L'opinion et la foule* (Paris: Alcan).

Taylor, D., (1998), "Critical review of psychotherapy services in England", *Psychoanalytic Psychotherapy*, 12, pp. 111–18.

Taylor, S. E., Wayment, H. A., and Collins, M. A. (1993), "Positive illusions and affect regulations", in D. M. Wegner and J. W. Pennebaker (eds), *Handbook of Mental Control* (Englewood Cliffs NJ: Prentice-Hall), pp. 325–43.

Thom R. (1990), *Parabole e catastrofi* (Milan: Il Saggiatore).

Varela, F. J. (1975), "A calculus for self-reference", *International Journal of General Systems*, 2, pp. 5–24.

Varela, F. J. (1979), *Principles of Biological Autonomy* (New York, NY: North Holland).

Varela, F. J. (1988), "Il circolo creativo: abbozzo di una storia naturale della circolarita", in P. Watzlawick, *La realtà inventata* (Milan: Feltrinelli).

Wampold, B. E. (2001), *The Great Psychotherapy Debate: Models, methods and findings* Mahwah, NJ: Erlbaum).

Watzlawick, P. (1976), *How Real is Real?* (New York, NY: Random House).

Watzlawick, P. (1977), *Die Möglichkeit des Andersseins: zur Technik der therapeutischen Kommunikation* (Bern: Verlag Hans Huber).

Watzlawick P. (ed) (1981), *Die Erfundene Wirklichkeit* (Munich: Piper und Co. Verlag).

Watzlawick, P. (1990a), "Therapy is what you say it is", in J. K. Zeig and S. G. Gilligan (eds), *Brief therapy: Myths, methods and metaphors* (New York, NY: Brunner/Mazel), pp. 55–61.

Watzlawick, P. (1990b), *Il codino del Barone di Münchhausen* (Milan: Feltrinelli).

Watzlawick, P., Beavin, J. H., and Jackson, Don D. (1967), *Pragmatics of Human Communication: A study of Interactional Patterns, Pathologies and Paradoxes* (New York, NY: W. W. Norton & Co.).

Watzlawick, P., and Nardone, G. (*a cura di*), (1997), *Terapia breve strategica* (Milan: Raffaello Cortina Editore).

Watzlawick, P., and Weakland, J. H. (1978), *La prospettiva relazionale* (Rome: Astrolabio).

Watzlawick, P., Weakland, J. H., and Fisch R. (1974), *Change: principles of problem formation and problem solution* (New York, NY: W. W. Norton & Co.).

Weakland, J. H., and Ray, W. A. (eds) (1995), *Propagations: thirty years of influence from the Mental Research Institute* (New York, NY: Haworth Press Inc.).

Weakland J. H., et al. (1974), "Brief Therapy: Focused Problem Resolution", in *Family Process*, XIII, pp. 141–68.

Weil, A. (1995), *Health and Healing* (New York, NY: Houghton Mifflin).

Weiss, B., and Weisz, J. R. (1990), "The impact of methodological factors on child psychotherapy outcome research: a meta-analysis for researchers", *Journal of Abnormal Child Psychology*, 18 (6), pp. 639–70.

Western, D., Novotny, C. M., and Thompson-Brenner, H. (2004a), "The Empirical Status of Empirically Supported Psychotherapies: Assumption, Findings and reporting in Controlled Clinical Trials", *Psychological Bulletin*, 130 (4), pp. 631–63.

Western, D., Novotny, C. M., and Thompson-Brenner, H. (2004b), "The next generation of psychotherapy research: Reply to Ablon & Marci (2004), Goldfried and Eubanks-Carter (2004) and Haag (2004)" *Psychological Bulletin*, 130 (4), pp. 677–83.

Whitehead, A. N., and Russel, B. (1910–13), *Principia Mathematica* (Cambridge, UK: Cambridge University Press).

Wiener N. (1967), *The Human Use of Human Being: cybernetics and society*, 2nd edn (New York, NY: Avon).

Wiener N. (1975), Cybernetics, or control and communication in the animal and the machine, Massachusetts Institute of Technology Press, Cambridge, II^a ed.

Wilde, O. (1986), *Aforismi* (Milan: Mondadori).

Wilson, D. B., and Lipsey, M. W. (2001), "The role of method in treatment effectiveness research", *Canadian Journal of Psychiatry*, 41 (7), pp. 421–8.

Wilson, G. (1998), "Manual-based treatment and clinical practice", *Clinical Psychology: Science and Practice*, 5, pp. 363–75.

Wittgenstein, L. (1980), *Remarks on the Philosophy of Psychology* (Oxford, UK: Basil Blackwell).

Wolpe, J. (1981) *Life Without Fear* (Oakland, CA: New Horlinger Publications).

Zeig, J. K. (1985), *Experiencing Erickson: an introduction to the man and his work* (New York, NY: Brunner Mazel).

Zeig, J. K. (1992), *The Evolution of Psychotherapy: The Second Conference* (New York, NY: Brunner Mazel).

Zeig, J. K., and Gilligan, S. (eds) (1990), *Brief Therapy: Myths, methods & metaphor* (New York, NY: Brunner Mazel).

Zimbardo, P. C. (1993), *Persuasion and Change* (New York, NY: Guilford).

Index

(page numbers in italic type refer to illustrations and "n" refers to footnotes)